Defoe Abbott Marx Hardy Melville Montaigne Machiavelli Chesterton Cooper Haggard Emerson Joyce Austen Hugo Eliot Grimm
Stoker Carroll Christie Maupassant Byron Molière Schiller
Wilde Garnett Einstein Fitzgerald Engels Smith Kafka Hall
Goethe Hawthorne Willis
Cotton Dostoyevsky
Baum Henry Kipling Doyle
Leslie Dumas Flaubert Turgenev Nietzsche Balzac
Stockton Vatsyayana Crane
Burroughs Verne
Curtis Tocqueville Gogol Vinci
Homer Widger Tolstoy Whitman Busch
Darwin Thoreau Twain
Potter Freud Zola Lawrence Scott Plato Harte
Kant Jowett Stevenson Dickens Burton Hesse
Andersen Cervantes
London Descartes Voltaire
Poe Aristotle Wells Cooke
Hale James Hastings
Bunner Shakespeare Irving
Richter Chri da Chambers
Doré Dante Chekhov Benedict Alcott
Swift Shaw Wodehouse Pushkin
Newton

 tredition®

tredition was established in 2006 by Sandra Latusseck and Soenke Schulz. Based in Hamburg, Germany, tredition offers publishing solutions to authors and publishing houses, combined with world-wide distribution of printed and digital book content. tredition is uniquely positioned to enable authors and publishing houses to create books on their own terms and without conventional manu-facturing risks.

For more information please visit: www.tredition.com

TREDITION CLASSICS

This book is part of the TREDITION CLASSICS series. The creators of this series are united by passion for literature and driven by the intention of making all public domain books available in printed format again - worldwide. Most TREDITION CLASSICS titles have been out of print and off the bookstore shelves for decades. At tredition we believe that a great book never goes out of style and that its value is eternal. Several mostly non-profit literature projects provide content to tredition. To support their good work, tredition donates a portion of the proceeds from each sold copy. As a reader of a TREDITION CLASSICS book, you support our mission to save many of the amazing works of world literature from oblivion. See all available books at www.tredition.com.

Project Gutenberg

The content for this book has been graciously provided by Project Gutenberg. Project Gutenberg is a non-profit organization founded by Michael Hart in 1971 at the University of Illinois. The mission of Project Gutenberg is simple: To encourage the creation and distribu-tion of eBooks. Project Gutenberg is the first and largest collection of public domain eBooks.

Bell's Cathedrals: The Cathedral Church of Salisbury A Description of its Fabric and a Brief History of the See of Sarum

Gleeson White

Imprint

This book is part of TREDITION CLASSICS

Author: Gleeson White
Cover design: Buchgut, Berlin – Germany

Publisher: tredition GmbH, Hamburg - Germany
ISBN: 978-3-8472-3025-0

www.tredition.com
www.tredition.de

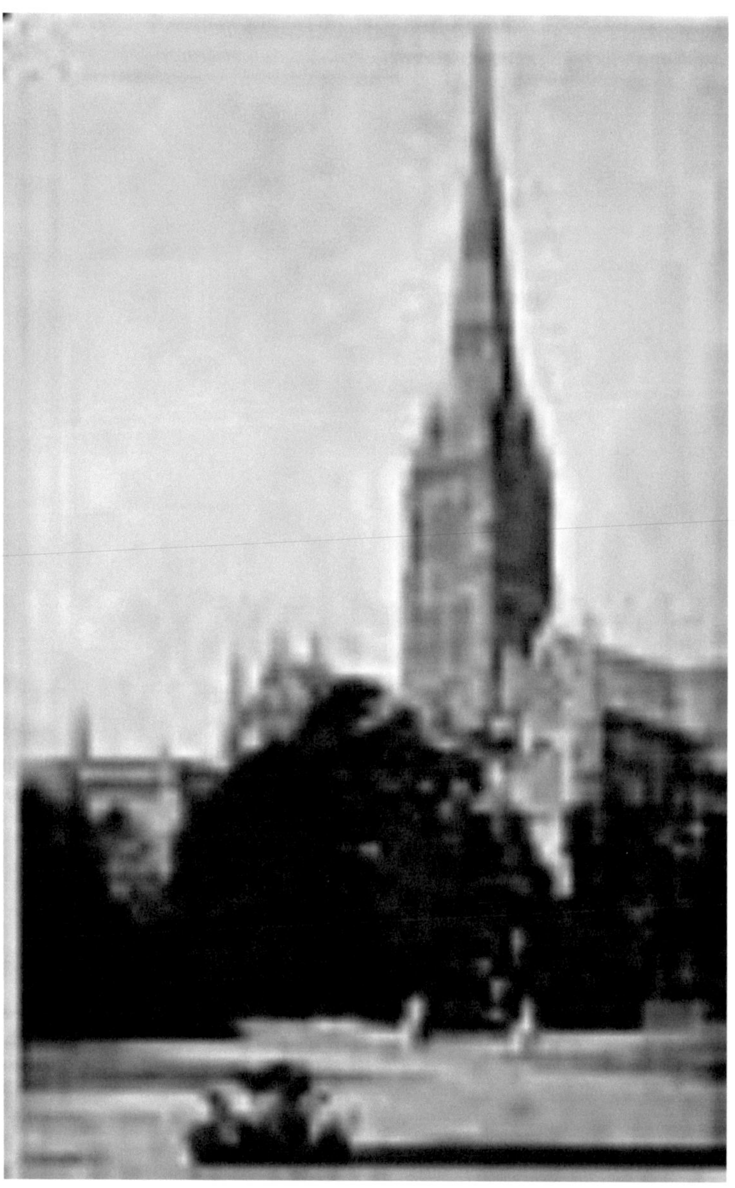

SALISBURY CATHEDRAL FROM THE BISHOP'S PALACE.

From a Photograph by Catherine Weed Ward. ToList

GENERAL PREFACE.

This series of monographs has been planned to supply visitors to the great English Cathedrals with accurate and well illustrated guide books at a popular price. The aim of each writer has been to produce a work compiled with sufficient knowledge and scholarship to be of value to the student of archæology and history, and yet not too technical in language for the use of an ordinary visitor or tourist.

To specify all the authorities which have been made use of in each case would be difficult and tedious in this place. But amongst the general sources of information which have been almost invariably found useful are:—firstly, the great county histories, the value of which, especially in questions of genealogy and local records, is generally recognized; secondly, the numerous papers by experts which appear from time to time in the transactions of the antiquarian and archæological societies; thirdly, the important documents made accessible in the series issued by the Master of the Rolls; fourthly, the well-known works of Britton and Willis on the English Cathedrals; and, lastly, the very excellent series of Handbooks to the Cathedrals, originated by the late Mr. John Murray, to which the reader may in most cases be referred for fuller detail, especially in reference to the histories of the respective sees.

Gleeson White.
Edward F. Strange.
Editors of the Series.

AUTHOR'S PREFACE.

The authorities consulted in the preparation of this book are too numerous to quote in detail. But the admirable works by the late Rev. W.H. Jones have been proved so full of useful information that the service they rendered must be duly acknowledged, although in almost every instance further reference was made to the building itself—or to officially authenticated documents. Nor must the help of one of the cathedral cicerones be overlooked, in spite of his desire to remain anonymous; for his knowledge of the building served to correct several mistakes in the first edition. One moot point concerning the bishop commemorated by an effigy in the North Choir Aisle is left an open question. Local authorities insist that it should be attributed to Bishop Poore, antiquarians of distinction affirm that it represents Bishop Bingham.

The illustrations, with the exception of a few details from Britton and Carter, are from photographs most courteously placed at my disposal by Mrs. H. Snowden Ward, or from the series published by Messrs. S.B. Bolas and Co., Carl Norman and Co. (now The Photochrom Company, Ltd.), Poulton and Sons (of Lee) and Witcomb and Son, of Salisbury, in each case duly acknowledged below the engraving.

G.W.

CONTENTS.

LIST OF ILLUSTRATIONS.

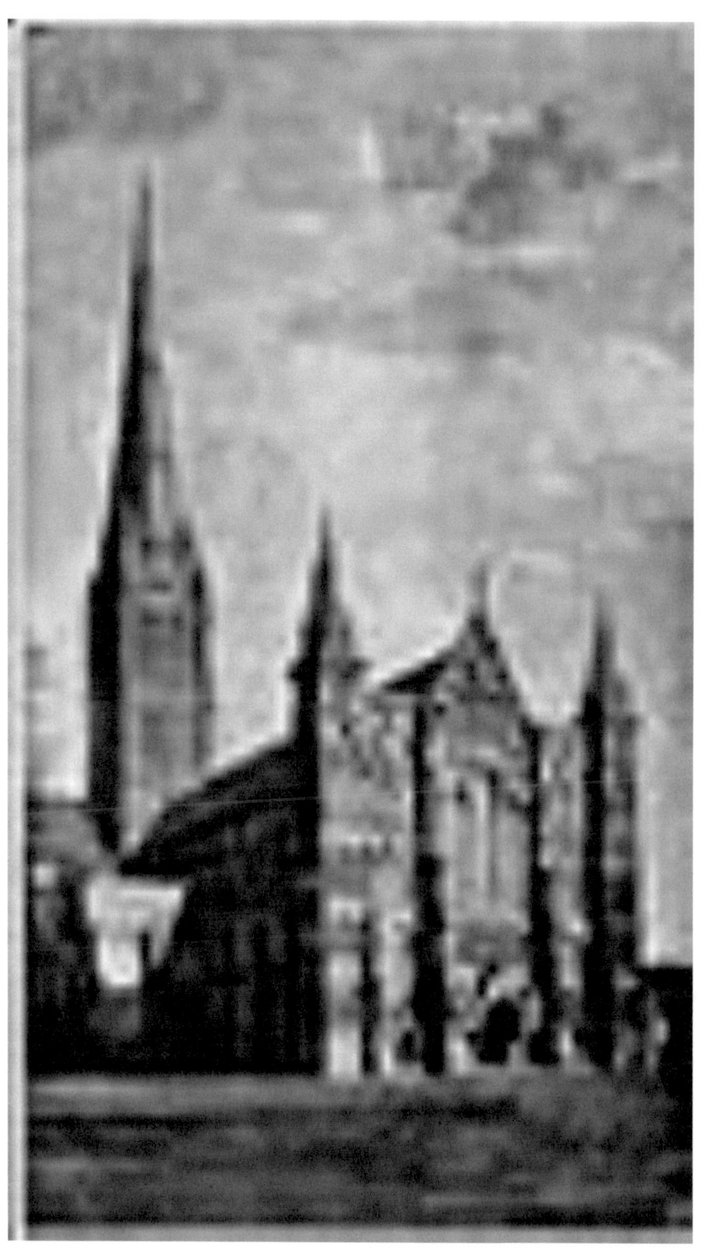

SALISBURY. THE WEST FRONT.
From a Photograph by Carl Norman and Co. ToList

[1]

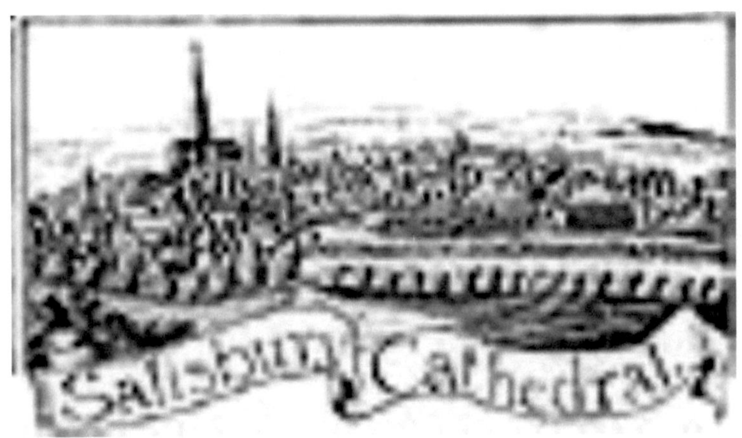

HISTORY OF THE CATHEDRAL CHURCH OF S. MARY.

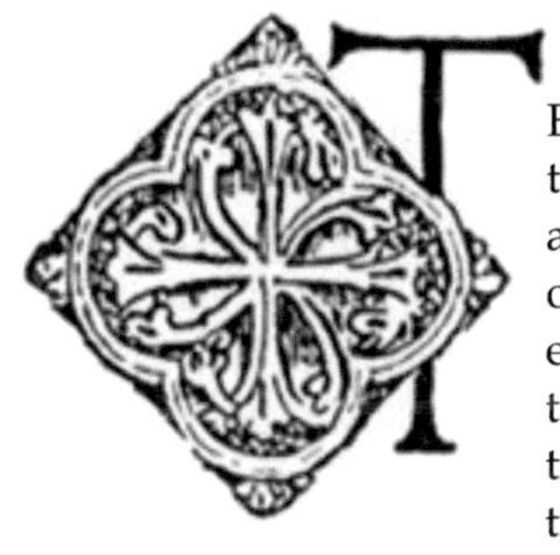

There is probably no cathedral church in Europe, certainly no other English one, that has such a clear record of its history as Salisbury. Whereas in almost every other instance we have only vague legendary accounts of the original foundation of the building, in this case there is a trustworthy chronicle of its first inception and each successive stage of its progress extant.

Owing to reasons noted in another chapter, the former cathedral at Old Sarum was condemned to be abandoned, and a new site chosen for its successor; Bishop Richard Poore, through whose efforts the change of locality was effected, is said to have hesitated long before he could find one suitable. Wilton, then a place of some importance, attracted him first. There is a more or less accurate MS. extant which professes to give an account of his tentative attempts to induce the Abbess of Wilton to permit him to build his church in a meadow of her domain. An old sewing-woman (*quaedam [2] vetula filatrix*) is said to have attributed his frequent visits to quite another motive; she inferred that the Bishop had a papal dispensation to marry, and was a suitor for the hand of the Abbess. The negotiations failed: "Hath not the Bishop land of his own that he must needs spoil the Abbess? Verily he hath many more sites on which he may build his church than this at Wilton," was the reply of the Abbess to his demand. During his period of indecision the Virgin appeared to him in a vision, and commanded him to build his new church in a place called Myr-field, or, as some accounts have it, Maer-field. He searched vainly for a piece of ground by that name, that he might obey the supernatural edict, until by chance he overheard a labourer (or a soldier, the legends vary,) talking of the Maer-field, and then having, as he thought, identified the place, which appears to have been within his own demesne, he commenced to plan the present building. Another tradition ignores the dream, and says the site of the cathedral was determined by an arrow shot from the ramparts of Old Sarum.

Misled by the similarity of sound, the name Maer-field has been, naturally enough, interpreted to mean Mary-field. The apparently obvious form "Miry-field," — as, according to Leland, it appears on an old inscription, — in spite of the marshy nature of the site, is probably a mere coincidence. Nor is Thomas Fuller's "Merry-field, for the pleasant situation thereof," better worth attention. The generally accepted theory at present is that *maer*, the Anglo-Saxon word for a boundary, supplies the clue. A hamlet, Marton, near Bedwin, another of the same name now corrupted to Martin, near Damerham, might each be truly described as boundary-towns. In Wiltshire to-day 'mere-stone' is the local idiom for a boundary-stone. Mere is alike the name of a hundred and of a parish in Wilts, both near its borders. The site of the present cathedral is at the junction of three ancient hundreds — Underditch, Alderbury, and Cawdon — the south-east wall of the close being the boundary line which divides the cathedral precincts from Cawdon.

Not only from the fact that the site was given by the bishop may we infer that the Poores were a wealthy family; but his brother Herbert, who was his immediate predecessor in the see, is described in the Osmund Register, as *dives et assiduus* (rich and painstaking), and Richard Poore before his enthronement was a benefactor to the monastery of Tarrant, in Dorsetshire, his native village. Later we find he gave a large estate at Laverstock to his new cathedral. Hence the old theory that his name was derived from Poor or Pauper, as it appears in several old chronicles, is untenable. Possibly like the Irish Poer or Power, it may be traced to the word *puer*, used in a restricted sense to denote the sons of royal or noble families not yet in possession of their heritage. A Prince of Wales in past times has been known as Puer Anglicanus, the Spanish "Infanta," the prefix "Childe," have all been cited in support of this theory. It is said indeed that the Childes trace their descent from the Le Poers, and Childe-Okeford and Poorstock, two villages in Dorset are quoted in evidence [2].

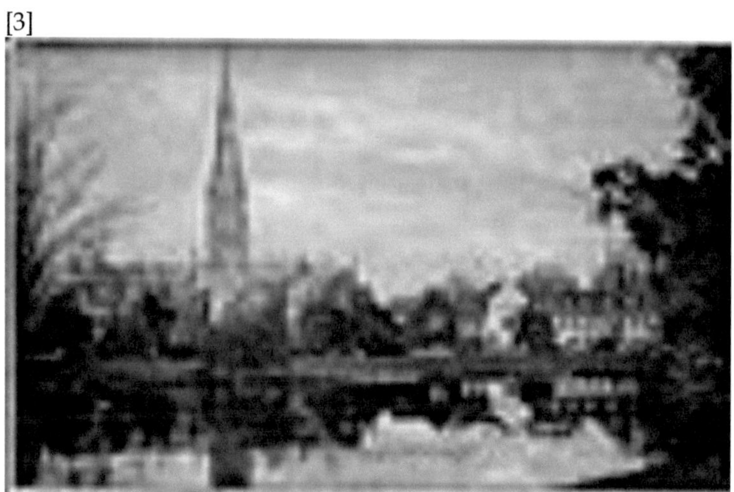

THE CATHEDRAL FROM THE SOUTH.
From a Photograph by Messrs. Poulton. ToList
[4]

[5] Whatever the origin of his name there is little doubt that the Bishop was wealthy, and absolute certainty that he was a powerful and capable ruler — the whole story of his successful efforts to carry out his scheme proves this much, were other testimony wanting. Even his choice of a site is justified by results, although earlier accounts unanimously agree in saying it was little better than a swamp. That such descriptions of the place were true is evident enough; the subsidence of the tower piers show that their foundation was insecure, and the curious feature of a continuous base to the piers of the nave prove also that provision was taken from the first to overcome this obstacle. We have frequent records of floods to the extent at times of causing the daily service to be suspended owing to the water actually being within the building itself; as late as 1763 there is an account of a specially high one thus interrupting the daily ritual. The whole valley of the Salisbury Avon to its seamouth at Christchurch, about twenty-nine miles distant is still under water for months at a time during a wet winter.

Of course the abundance of water has evoked the usual comparison with Venice. Thomas Fuller, who for the sake of his usual sagacity may be forgiven an allusion so unfounded, says: "This mindeth me of an epitaph made on Mr. Francis Hill, a native of Salisbury, who died secretary to the English liege at Venice — 'Born in the English Venice, thou did'st die, dear Friend, in the Italian Salisbury.'"

[6] One of the reasons most frequently alleged for the abandonment of Old Sarum was its lack of water; but if it was deemed unadvisable to acknowledge the political and administrative reasons which really decided the change, it is just possible that the superfluity of water was found useful as a plausible explanation of the removal on hygienic grounds; or it may even be that the whole story of the scarcity of water at Old Sarum was a later invention to excuse its unwelcome abundance in the new locality. Bishop Douglas is credited with the saying, "Salisbury is the sink of Wiltshire plain, the close is the sink of Salisbury, and the bishop's palace the sink of the close." Certainly the site lacks the natural dignity of position such an edifice demands, and which Lincoln, Durham, Ely, and many another English cathedral, show was frequently deemed essential. Thomas Fuller, who occupied a stall at Salisbury, has written, "The most curious and cavilling eye can desire nothing in this edifice except an ascent, seeing such as address themselves hither can hardly say with David, 'I will go up to the house of the Lord.'"

The temporary chapel of wood, commenced on the Monday after Easter in 1219, must have been a modest structure, since on the next Trinity Sunday the Bishop celebrated mass, and the same day consecrated a cemetery there.

In the MS. by William de Wanda, precentor and afterwards dean of Sarum, preserved in the Cathedral Library, we have a record of the very first ceremonies connected with the Cathedral, which being probably trustworthy in the main is so curiously interesting in itself, that it deserves quoting freely, from the version given by Francis Price, clerk of the works to the Cathedral, and author of a very interesting monograph upon it, published in the latter part of the last century. We find that in the year A.D. 1220, on the day of St. Vitalis the Martyr, being the fourth of the calends of May (which was the twenty-eighth of April), the foundations were laid by Bishop Richard Poore. "On the day appointed for the purpose the bishop came with great devotion, few earls or barons of the county, but a great multitude of the common people coming in from all parts; and when divine service had been performed, and the Holy Spirit invoked, the said bishop, putting off his shoes, went in procession with the clergy of the church to the place of foundation singing the litany; then the litany being [7] ended and a sermon first made to the people, the bishop laid the first stone for our Lord the Pope Honorius, and the second for the Lord Stephen Langton, Archbishop of Canterbury and Cardinal of the Holy Roman Church, at that time with our Lord the King in the Marches of Wales; then he added to the new fabric a third stone for himself; William Longespée, Earl of Sarum, who was then present, laid the fourth stone, and Elaide [3] Vitri, Countess of Sarum, the wife of the said earl, a woman truly pious and worthy because she was filled with the fear of the Lord, laid the fifth. After her certain noblemen, each of them added a stone; then the dean, the chantor, the chancellor, the archdeacons and canons of the church of Sarum who were present did the same, amidst the acclamations of multitudes of the people weeping for joy and contributing thereto their alms with a ready mind according to the ability which God had given them. But in process of time the nobility being returned from Wales, several of them came thither, and laid a stone, binding themselves to some special contribution for the whole seven years following."

Another account, differing from the more generally accepted version just quoted, says that: Pendulph, the Pope's legate, in 1216 laid the first five stones; the first for the Pope, the second for the King, the third for the Earl of Salisbury, the fourth for the countess, and the fifth for the bishop. This statement is wrong in date, for Bishop Poore was not translated to the see of Sarum until the year 1217. In the charter of Henry I. the first stone is mentioned as having been laid by the king, *i.e.*, in his name.

"On the 15th of August, 1220, at a general chapter when the bishop was present, it was provided that if any canon of the church failed paying what he had promised to the fabric for seven years, that next after fifteen days from the term elapsed, some one should be sent on the part of the bishop and chapter to raise what was due from the corn found on the prebend, and so long as he should remain there for that purpose he should be maintained with all necessaries by the goods of the said prebend. But if the prebend or any person failing in the payment of what was promised be in any other bishopric than Sarum, such canon should be denounced to that bishop by the letter of the bishop and chapter for his contumacy, either to be suspended from entering the church, or from celebration of [8] divine service, or excommunicated according as the chapter shall judge it."

In the year 1225, Richard Poore, Bishop of Sarum, "finding the fabric of the new church was by God's alliance so far advanced that divine service might be conveniently performed therein, he rejoiced exceedingly, since he bestowed great pains and contributed greatly towards it. Thereupon he commanded William the Dean to cite all the canons to be present on the day of S. Michael following, at the joyful solemnity of their mother church, that is to say, at the first celebration of divine service therein. According on the vigil of S. Michael, which happened on a Sunday, the bishop came in the morning and consecrated three altars, the first in the east part, in honour of the holy and undivided Trinity and All Saints, on which henceforth the mass of the Blessed Virgin was appointed to be said every day. And the said bishop offered that day for the service of the said altar and for daily service of the Blessed Virgin, two silver basons and two silver candlesticks which were bequeathed by the will of the noble lady Gundria de Warren to the church of Sarum. Moreover the bishop gave out of his property to the clerks that were to officiate at the said mass thirty marks of silver a year until he settled so much in certain rents, and likewise ten marks every year to maintain lamps round the said altar. Then he dedicated another altar in the north part of the church in honour of St. Peter, the prince of the apostles, and the rest of the apostles; he also dedicated another altar in the south part thereof to St. Stephen and the rest of the martyrs. At this dedication were present: Henry, Bishop of Dublin, Stephen, Lord Archbishop of Canterbury."

We read further in the same chronicle that the bishops and their retinues were entertained for a week by Bishop Poore at his sole charge.

The next day, the feast of SS. Michael and All Angels, the Archbishop of Canterbury preached to a large company including many English and foreign prelates, Otto, the Pope's nuncio, and others. On the Thursday following, "Our Lord the King and Hubert de Burgh the justice came to the church and the King there heard the mass of the glorious Virgin and offered ten marks of silver and one piece of silk, and he granted to the same place that every year there should be a fair." The same day the justice made a vow that he would give a gold [9] text set in the precious stones and the relics of divers saints in honour of the Blessed Virgin Mary, and the service of the new church; afterwards the King went down with many of his nobles to the Bishop's palace and were entertained. On the Friday following Hubert de Burgh offered his "texte after John, gilt with gold and having precious stones and relics of divers saints."

"On the Nativity of our Lord following, the King and his justice Hubert de Burgh came to Sarum on the day of the Holy Innocents, and there the King offered one gold ring with a precious stone called a ruby, one piece of silk, and one gold cup of the weight of ten marks; and when the mass was celebrated the King told the dean that he would have that stone which he had offered and the gold of the ring applied to adorn the text which the justice had before given; and then the justice caused the text which he had given to be brought and offered with great devotion on the altar."

On the 10th of January, 1226, William Longespée, Earl of Salisbury, returned from Gascoigne, where he had resided twelve months with Richard, the King's brother, for the defence of Bordeaux (after three months on the channel between the Isle of Rhè and the coast of Cornwall, owing to the tempestuous weather, that so long delayed his landing), "and the said Earl came that day after nine o'clock to Sarum, where he was received with great joy, with a procession for the new fabric." The scandalous account of his death (as given by Stow), which occurred at the castle of Old Sarum, on the 7th of March in the same year, and the part played in the transaction by Hubert de Burgh cannot be told here, beyond the fact that the justice was strongly suspected of poisoning him. On the 8th of March, at the same hour of the day on which he had been received with great joy, he was brought to New Sarum with many tears and lamentations, and honourably buried in the new church of the

Blessed Virgin. Matthew Paris gravely records that at his funeral, despite gusts of wind and rain, the candles furnished a continual light the whole of the way. Of all secular figures connected with this cathedral his is perhaps the most prominent, nor is his fame merely local. He was active in public affairs during the reign of King John, and one of the noticeable heroes in an expedition to the Holy Land in 1220, when, at the battle of Damietta, Matthew Paris tells us, he [10] resisted the shock of the infidels like a wall. He fought both in Flanders and in France, was at his King's side at Runnymede, and a witness to Magna Charta — a copy of which famous charter, made probably for his special use, is still preserved in the cathedral library.

In 1226, on the Feast of the Holy Trinity, which was then the 18th day of the calends of July, the bodies of the three bishops, Jocelin, Roger, and Osmund (the latter not yet canonized), were brought from Old Sarum. Whether their tombs were also brought, is not said, nor is any mention made of Herman, who by popular report is credited with a monument in the cathedral.

A Charter of Henry III., dated 30th of January, 1227, gives certain powers to make new roads and bridges, to inclose the city of New Saresbury, to institute a fair from the Vigil of the Assumption of the Blessed Mary to the octave of the same feast, etc., etc. This development of the city, more especially by its roads and bridges, is held to have been fatal to the prosperity of Wilton, which from that time ceased to progress, and was over-shadowed by the now rapidly increasing New Sarum.

Bishop Poore was ably supported in his great undertaking by a group of notable men, among whom were: William de Wanda, the Dean, who threw his whole soul into the work, and traversed the diocese of London to collect alms in its behalf, besides leaving us most elaborate accounts of the various ceremonies; and the Precentor, Roger de Sarum, a man of some weight, who soon after became Bishop of Bath and Wells; Henry de Bishopston, a learned man and a scholar, should also be remembered, and, if Leland could be credited, we should need to add another member to this group, and find in Robert Hilcot, of Sarum, the author of the "Philobiblon" so generally attributed to Richard de Bury.

After Bishop Poore was translated to Durham, his three successors, Bishops Robert Bingham (1229-1246), William of York (1247-1256), and Giles of Bridport (1257-1262), continued the works of the new building with great energy. In 1258 it was consecrated—some accounts say by Bishop Giles of Bridport, "who covered the roof throughout with lead," but more probably by Boniface of Savoy, Archbishop of Canterbury. Henry III. and his queen were present at the consecration; and as indulgences of a year and forty days were offered to all who should be present during the octave of the dedication, vast [11] crowds visited it. It was not entirely completed according to a note in a Book of Statutes, until 1266, and it has been said that with all our modern appliances we could hardly shorten the forty-six years it occupied. The cost of the whole building, according to ancient authority, was about 40,000 marks, equal to £26,666 13s. 4d., of the money of that day, and probably equivalent roughly to half a million in our own time. Among many benefactors, one, Lady Alicia Bruere, who according to Leland contributed the marble and stone for twelve years, deserves to be mentioned. The cloisters and chapter house were not commenced until the episcopate of Bishop Walter de la Wyle (1263-1271) and possibly not completed until some ten years later. From the will of Robert de Careville, the treasurer in 1267, we find that there were seven altars in the church at this date; he bequeathed seven pounds to provide fourteen silver phials (each bearing a representation of three keys) in order that each altar might have two. The erection of the spire, evidently not included in the original plan, is often erroneously assigned to Wyville (1336-1375), who certainly completed the wall of the close, and enlarged the cloisters. The King granted him a charter for this purpose, and also gave him the stones of the old Cathedral, many of which, with the Norman work upon them, may be seen plainly at the present time. (See p. 22.)

It is interesting to note that not only is Salisbury the most complete example of its period in this country, but is also the first important building carried out entirely in the style we now know as early English. Henry III. is believed to have been so enthusiastic in his admiration of Bishop Poore's new Cathedral that he set about the rebuilding of Westminster Abbey, which was commenced in 1245 and completed in 1269, as far as the east end of the choir. The early English work at Salisbury has a certain poverty of detail when compared with Westminster, and the "Angel Choir" of Lincoln undoubtedly surpasses both; yet the effect of Salisbury has a character of its own and a purity in its ornament that is in itself a distinction. The Cathedral of Amiens, of exactly the same date, covers 71,000 square feet, Salisbury but 55,000; the vault of Amiens is 152 feet high, Salisbury only 85; but, as Fergusson observes in his "Handbook of Architecture," the fair mode of comparison is to ask whether the Cathedral of Amiens is finer than Salisbury would be if the latter were at least twice as large as it is.

[12] There has long been a tradition that Elias de Dereham was the architect of this stately pile, and the information gathered together by the Rev. J.A. Bennet, in a paper read before the British Archæological Association at Salisbury on August 5th, 1887, certainly does much to strengthen the belief. From this account, and other sources, we find that Elias de Derham is first mentioned in the Rot. Chartarum, Ap. 6 (6 John, 1208)? where he is described as one of the King's clerks and Rector of Meauton. In 1206 he appears to have been a royal official. In 1209 he is reported to have been the architect for the repairs of King John's palace at Westminster. In 1212 he attached himself to the opposite party, but was taken again into the King's favour in the following year. We have specially interesting notice of his work in 1220, when he was engaged upon the shrine of St. Thomas at Canterbury. Matthew Paris, in his account of the translation of St. Thomas, distinctly states that the shrine was the work of that incomparable officer, Walter de Colchester, Sacrist of St. Albans, assisted by Elias de Dereham, Canon of Salisbury. Leland mentions, in an extract from an old "Martyrologie" of Salisbury, that he was rector — or director — of the new church for twenty-five years from the beginning, whether he means architect or clerk of the works is not so clear. His name, as one of the Canons of the Cathedral, occurs eleven times in the "Osmund Register" at Salisbury. There are also references to him in the "Book of Evidences" (Liber Evidentiarum) among the bishop's muniments, as the builder of the original Aula Plumbea — Leden-hall — a famous old house in the close. The document is entitled *"Scriptura de domibus de Leden-hall per Eliam de Dereham sumptuose constructis,"* "a deed concerning the house called Leden-hall, built at great expense by Elias

de Dereham." This residence house remained six centuries after in the gift of the Bishop of Sarum.

During the year in which he accompanied Bishop Poore in his translation to Durham, and from 1230 to 1238, he was employed upon some architectural work connected with Durham Cathedral, which, when Bishop Poore accepted it was a stately Norman fane with an apsidal choir; he removed this east end, and remodelled it in the early English manner. The chapel of the Nine Altars, as this portion is called, is remarkably similar in its details to much of the work at Salisbury. It is curious that two southern churches so near as Salisbury and [13] Christchurch Priory should be found influencing or influenced by the great northern cathedral, but the likeness between Flambard's Norman work at Christchurch and the same bishop's work at Durham is as strongly marked as the Early English of Bishop Poore at both the churches in which he was enthroned. That Elias de Dereham is responsible for much of the work of both cathedrals is also a fair assumption. Curiously enough his name, hitherto hastily assumed to be equivalent to Elias of Durham, has probably no connection with that city; whether, however, his patronym should be traced to the Norfolk Dereham, or the Gloucester Dyrham, it is impossible to say with any certainty. On somewhat insufficient grounds it has been hazarded that his portrait may be found in a figure on the east side of the staircase buttress of what was formerly the great entrance to Wells Cathedral.

Owing to the fact that the original design of the building was fully carried out, with the addition of a tower and spire, its architectural history ceases just where most others begin their chequered career. At the time of the Reformation it suffered but little, except in the wholesale destruction of its stained glass. Dr. Pope, in his "Life of Bishop Ward," says that even during the Civil War, when it was abandoned, workmen were engaged to keep it in repair, who when questioned as to the authority by which they worked, said, "Those who employ'd us will pay us; trouble not your selves to inquire who they are. Whoever they are, they do not desire to have their names known." We find as evidence of the secret influence exerted in its behalf that when one of Waller's officers sent up to the Parliament certain plate and a pulpit cloth from Salisbury Cathedral, he was ordered to restore them, as it was considered that he had overstepped his commission; all that was retained being certain copes, hangings, and a picture of the Virgin.

At the Restoration, Bishop Ward, after a great thunderstorm in 1668, when fears were entertained for the safety of the spire, called in Sir Christopher Wren, who, after examining the tower, expressed his belief "that a spire was not contemplated by its builders;" that "out of fear to overburden the four piers of the tower, its inside was carried for 40 feet above the nave with a slender hollow work of pillars and arches, nor hath it any buttresses; the spire itself is but 9 inches thick, though the height be above 150 feet." This work of pillars and arches led him to [14] conclude that the architect laid his first floor of timber 40 feet higher than the vault beneath.

Dr. Walter Pope, in his "Life of Bishop Seth Ward," 1697, describes the restorations accomplished by this excellent prelate: "There being, therefore, not much to be done as to reparation, he employ'd himself in the Decoration of the Cathedral: First, at his proper charges Paving the Cloyster. I mean that side of it which leads out of his garden into the church. At his exhortation, and more than proportinable (*sic*) expence the Pavement of the Church was mended where it was faulty, and the whole Quire laid with white and black squares of marble. The Bishops, Deans, and all the Prebendaries Stalls made New & Magnificent, and the whole church was kept so clean, that anyone who had occasion for Dust to throw on the Superscription of a Letter, he would have a hard task to find it there.... His next care was to repair, I might almost say rebuild his Palace, which was much ruined, the Hall being pulled down, & the Greater part of the House converted to an Inn ... what remained of the Palace was divided into small Tenements and let out to poor Handicraft-men. This dilapidation was the work of one Van Ling, a Dutchman, by trade a Taylor, who bought it of Parliament when Bishop's lands were exposed to sale."

In the minutes of the chapter for August 26th, 1789, we find instruction given to Wyatt "to make new Canopies to the Stalls, to build a new Pulpit and Bishop's Throne, to put new Iron Rails to the Communion, with coping thereon, and set new blue stone steps to receive the same, to put two Wainscot Screens across the Aisles, to lay blue stone paving in the Lady Chapel, in squares to be cut out of the old gravestones, and enrich the side walls according to the drawings, to clean and colour the church from the East end of the Transept, and make the Screen to the Western Side of the organ." They also ordered "the beam in the choir to be removed, the North and South Porches to be taken down, the south door near the Verger's house stopped up, and another opened near the Chapter Vestry, to open out the Chapel in the great North and South Transepts, and to convert the north-east transept into a morning chapel, to remove certain monuments in consequence of alterations in St. Mary's Chapel, & to take down the Beauchamp & Hungerford Chapels, on the plea that they were in a state as to greatly [15] exceed any ordinary or possible means of repair." These formal instructions were not merely obeyed but exceeded, and the demolitions of that time confront the student of the building in all his researches. Of late years many minor alterations have been carried out, with a view to restore monuments to their original site, and, as far as possible, to obliterate Wyatt's damage; but the two superb chantries, the bell tower, the painted glass, and many other important features are hopelessly effaced, and the cathedral, spared by its avowed foes, has met with its greatest disaster from the hands of former guardians.

For the last thirty years the work of restoration has been gradually carried on until its recent completion. An arrangement was made in 1862 by which the Ecclesiastical Commissioners permitted the Dean and Chapter to spend £10,000 on the building, as part of a payment in lieu of transfer of their property. Sir G. Gilbert Scott had control of the restoration. Owing to the necessary work proving far more costly than the sum allowed was able to effect, a public meeting was held, subscriptions were started, and ultimately sufficient money raised to repair thoroughly the exterior of the building. The tower and spire were strengthened by an ingenious system of iron ties planned by Mr. Shields, the well-known engineer. The west front was restored, and more than sixty statues placed in its vacant niches. In the interior the Lady Chapel was restored, and its floor laid with encaustic tiles from the designs of ancient examples in various parts of the cathedral. The walls were cleaned, and the paintings of the roof reproduced by Messrs. Clayton and Bell. The choir was restored in memory of Bishop Hamilton, and the old choir stalls cleared. The organ-screen built by Wyatt out of fragments of the Hungerford and Beauchamp chapels was removed. Throughout the building the Purbeck marble shafts have been most carefully preserved and repolished. Besides this much decorative work of various sorts, including some excellent examples of modern stained glass and metal work, has been added from time to time. At present the interior has less obvious evidence of age than any other English building of its date, but for this the modern restorer is not entirely responsible, as Wyatt rendered much alteration needful, and the design of the work has, as we have remarked elsewhere, a curiously modern quality in its finish and symmetry which is apt to mislead a casual observer.

FOOTNOTES:

[1] The headpiece is from an engraving in Walpoole's "British Traveller."

[2] A paper on this subject was printed in the Wiltshire Archæological Mag., No. lvi.

[3] So misspelt in the text quoted.

[16]

THE CATHEDRAL—EXTERIOR.

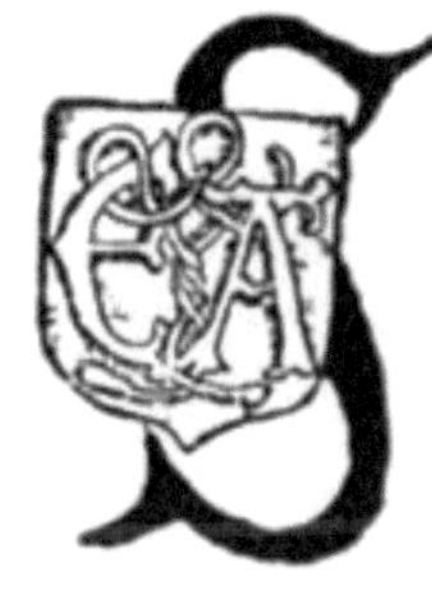

alisbury stands alone among English cathedrals for unity of design. To own its possession of this quality, which is undoubtedly both the earliest and the most mature impression the cathedral imparts, is by no means equivalent to unqualified praise. There are buildings of equal and less importance, whence illustrations might be taken for a complete history of every period of Gothic architecture; here the examples would be limited not only to one style, but if we except the upper stories of the tower and its spire, the cloisters, and a few minor additions, to a very restricted use of Early English, as it was practised from A.D. 1220 to 1258.

Another uncommon feature not so apparent at first sight, but yet almost, if not quite as rare, is that the present building was erected on a virgin site. It is hard to find a mediæval church of any importance in England that is not only upon the self-same site, but more often in part upon the actual foundation of an earlier edifice. Consistency is the especial character of Salisbury, and now, owing to Wyatt's iconoclastic destruction of the two later chapels at its east end, we have in Salisbury "the most typical English cathedral," which is also our most complete example of Early English.

That this artistic unity is as interesting as a design subsequently modified by other influences, may be an open question. There are those who think Salisbury "faultily faultless, icily regular, splendidly null," yet they would hardly dare to continue the quotation and say it was "dead perfection, no more." Even at a time when mediæval art was not generally appreciated in England, this cathedral won admiration from chance visitors such as Evelyn, who saw it in July, 1654, and pronounced it [17] "the completest Gothic work in Europe." Pepys, who also left his impressions of it, says: "The minster most admirable, as big I think and handsomer than Westminster, and a most large close about it and offices for the officers thereof, and a fine palace for the bishop." In later times Motley, the historian, thought it "too neat." Henry James calls it "a blonde beauty among churches," and even hints that it is a little banal. Another American critic, Mrs. Van Rensselaer, in a sympathetic study of the cathedral which appeared in "The Century Magazine," says: "If we think it feeble, it will be because we cannot see strength where it has been brought to perfect poise and ease. If our verdict is 'banal,' it will be because we cannot tell the commonplace from the simply and exactly right, or we do not know how rare the latter is — because we long for eccentricity as a proof of personality, and need what the French call *emphase* to impress us; there is no over-emphasis about Salisbury, neither in its effect as a whole, nor in any of its parts, neither in its design, nor in its treatment. But just in this fact lies its greatest merit, and just by reason of this fact, joined to its mighty size and its exceptional unity, it is intensely individual, personal, distinct from all other churches in the world."

Dean Stanley, in comparing it with Westminster Abbey, hardly overpraised it in saying: "Salisbury is all-glorious without, Westminster is all-glorious within." Canon Venables considers it "as an architectural composition, more especially as seen from the outside, the most perfectly designed building in the world." Elsewhere he speaks of it as "presenting none of those architectural problems so baffling and perplexing at Canterbury, Lichfield, or Lincoln." Its appearance from a distance has been the theme of poets, and a favourite subject for artists. Constable especially delighted to paint it. Among several of his different versions of the theme, the view from the meadows (with the rainbow), made popular by Lucas' mezzotint, is perhaps the best known.

Studying the building more closely one feels it is not accident that gives to it its peculiar charm, but pre-arranged design; the idea of one conception carried to its logical completion. This striking unity (despite the afterthought of the spire) certainly helps to impart an air of modernity to the building, that is lacking in far less ancient work, for oddly [18] enough it is often the decaying features of the latest decorated style that impress the vulgar by their apparent age. The extreme care in the masonry has imparted a machine-like finish. As Professor Willis wrote: "The regularity of the size of the stones is astonishing. As soon as they had finished one part, they copied it exactly in the next, even though the additional expense was considerable. The masonry runs in even bands, and you may follow it from the south transept, eastward, round to the north transept, after which they have not taken such great pains in their regularity. It is almost impossible to distinguish where they could have left off, for it is hardly to be supposed they could have gone on with all at the same time."

If at first sight this regular and symmetrical detail offers a suspicion of mere mechanism, yet it is no less evident that after longer study the charms of this exquisite structure tell with a lasting power. Too subtle to extort admiration at first, it bewitches a student of architecture who notes the scholarly reticence of its detail, the masterly way in which, as a rule, the construction is legitimately ornamented and the decoration made an integral part of the whole design.

[19]

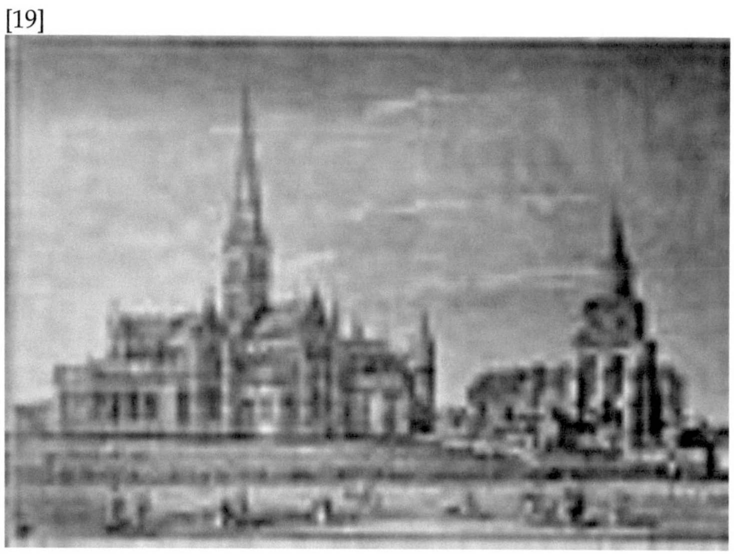

SALISBURY CATHEDRAL AND BELL TOWER.
From an Old Engraving. ToList
[20]

The Tower, with its famous spire, needs no apologist to justify its claim to be considered the most beautiful, not merely in England, but in Europe. From the time Leland naïvely wrote, "the tower of stone and the high pyramis of stone on it is a noble and memorable 'peace' of work," every critic of the cathedral praises the tower unreservedly, although Defoe was anxious to improve it, for he said: "The beauty of it is hurt by a thing easily to be remedied, which is this. The glass in the several windows being very old, has contracted such a rust, that it is scarcely to be distinguished from the stone walls; consequently, it appears as if there were no lights at all in the tower, but only recesses in the stone, whereas could the windows be glazed with squares and kept clean, which might be done, they would be plainly visible at a distance, and not only so, but from the adjacent hills you would see the light quite through the tower, which would have a very fine effect." It is curious to remember that perfectly as it accords with the rest of the pile, so that it seems the very central motive of the whole scheme, yet it is really an addition. Like the touch of genius which by one word changes [21] a good poem to a flawless lyric, so the creator of this crown to an already beautiful building by his final touch seems to have imparted additional beauty to that which already existed. The first idea was doubtless to add a lantern after the style of Ely, or at most a wooden spire. That the lower part of the tower is part of the original design, and intended to be open to the church, is proved by the presence of a series of detached Purbeck marble columns in the style of the rest of the internal masonry, which, hidden by the groining, or half-concealed by later masonry, were obviously meant to be part of the decoration of the interior, but again, the original plan of the tower made no provision for the huge weight of a stone spire. Indeed, it is quite doubtful if in its first state it was able to support itself, for curiously designed abutments are built in the triforium and clere-story of the nave, choir, or transepts on each of its four sides. The stonework of these is Early English, which if slightly later than the first story of the tower, is yet considerably earlier than its two upper stories. Notwithstanding the faulty construction that needed additional work so soon after it was erected, about fifty years later a daring architect super-imposed two stories, and added the lofty spire, which still stands, despite an early settlement which deflected it 23 inches out of the perpendicular. But its stability can hardly be reckoned a tribute to the judgment of the architect, for many times since complex arrangements of iron bands and ties have been added to ward off such a disaster as that which lost Chichester its spire in 1861, and has caused many others to be rebuilt from the very foundations. By a report of Sir Christopher Wren made in the time of Bishop Seth Ward, two hundred years ago, it is evident that in his time the deflection was not increasing, nor do quite recent observations show any reason for serious anxiety. This haunting fear, however, has led to curiously precise experiments for ascertaining the state of the spire. Francis Price, at the end of the last century, describes many of these, especially one carried out in the presence of the bishop, on July 18th, 1717; he also illustrates an elaborate system of additional bands and ties in his time. During the restorations that were begun in 1863, a further arrangement of iron bands, planned by Mr. Shields, the engineer, was introduced into the lantern story of the tower.

Parker, in his "Glossary," believes the date of the spire to [22] be about 1300; other authorities fix it thirty years later. Certain deeds in the "Book of Evidences" preserved among the Cathedral muniments show that in 1326 Edward III. granted a license for surrounding the close with a wall, and in 1331 authorized the bishop and canons to use the stones of the church of Old Sarum for that purpose. But against the theory that the material thus obtained was used in the tower also, there is the patent fact that while on many stones in the wall there are traces of Norman mouldings and other evidence of former use, neither in the tower nor spire do the stones betray any such origin. Modern antiquaries are wellnigh agreed upon the earlier dates; for in the Capitular Register, begun in 1329, there is no mention of the spire, which could hardly have escaped record had so important a work been then in progress. In support of this theory it is urged that from 1258 to 1297 the deans were men who took great interest in the fabric and are entered in its calendar of benefactors. Three of these became successively Bishops of Salisbury. But the deans who were appointed after 1297 were chiefly foreigners, several being cardinals and relatives of the Pope, whose duties elsewhere would have left them little but a purely temporal interest in the building. One of them, Peter of Savoy, was in conflict with his bishop, and evaded an episcopal admonition ordering him to residence.

Bishop Godwin, in his "Catalogue of Bishops," notes that in 1258 the cathedral was rehallowed by Boniface, Archbishop of Canterbury, and this fact is the basis of most of the argument for the earlier date of the spire, the completion of which, according to some, could alone have justified the ceremony.

Remembering that Winchester had lost its central tower, which fell in 1107, we can understand the reasons which induced the original architect to distrust a spire, and to adopt a lantern in its place. If, however, timidity delayed it at first, when it was undertaken, its builder left it not only the most lofty in England then and since, but in actual effect the most lofty in the world. This is claimed in spite of its 404 feet being exceeded by Amiens (422 feet), and Strasburg (488 feet), and although it might appear special pleading to urge such a theory against contradictory facts, yet since at Amiens the nave roof is 208 feet high, against the 115 feet of Salisbury, it is [23] obvious that the apparent height of the latter exceeds its French rival. At Strasburg the excess of elaboration in the ornament is detrimental to the effect of height, and the same may be said of Antwerp or Mechlin, where the whole effect is not so much that of a spire, as of an elaborately fretted finial, insubstantial if exquisite in itself, but merely an added ornament, not appearing part of the solid structure.

Despite the somewhat ornate details of the upper stories and spire, they accord well with the rest of the building, and, although typical Early Decorated of the time of Edward III., fail to clash with the more severe Early English work. These two stories have elaborately canopied arcades running round them, the windows being pierced through two of the arches on each façade and not emphasized by any special treatment. Above each story is a traceried parapet of lozenge decoration, the same design being repeated in the two bands that encircle the spire itself. At each of the four angles of the tower is an octagonal turret with crocketed spire. Amid a coronet of decorated finials the great octagonal spire grows naturally with no abrupt revelation of its change of plan. The whole cresting of the tower, and the perfectly natural way in which its lines continue easily into the graceful spire itself, are triumphs of successful design. The silhouette of the mass against the sky so precisely reaches the ideal effect that it is difficult to restrain oneself to sober criticism in describing it, yet the result is achieved so naturally that until we compare it with others, especially with modern ones, we hardly do justice to the subtle beauty that gives it a right to the supremacy it has won. The timber framework erected as a scaffold during the progress of the building still remains inside the spire and helps to impart strength to it; those curious in such matters will find a mass of information and many plans and drawings of its internal construction in Francis Price's "Antiquities of Salisbury, 1774." In 1762, during the progress of some repairs to the capstone and the addition of a new copper vane, the workmen discovered a wooden box, and inside it a round leaden one 5-½ inches in diameter and 2-¼ inches deep, which contained a piece of woven fabric. [4] This was conjectured to be a relic of the Virgin Mary, the patron saint of the church, which had been deposited there to guard the lofty spire from danger by lightning or tempest. When tested on the 600th anniversary of the [24] building the spire showed, it is said, no further deflection from that registered two centuries earlier. Consequently the settlement in the two western piers being so long at a standstill, and the repeated additions of metal work to strengthen the spire being apparently entirely successful, there seemed no reason to doubt but that in the natural course of events it would remain for many centuries a landmark to its neighbourhood and one of the greatest triumphs of English mediæval workmanship. [5] Richard de Farley, a Wiltshire man, is supposed to have been the architect of the spire; that his artistic instinct was right is evident today, but his engineering foresight seems less certain, as in all probability the settlement began almost immediately after the erection. Indeed it is said that the efforts to obtain the canonization of Osmund were started in 1387 to increase the popularity of the cathedral as a place of pilgrimage, and thereby to augment its revenue, so that funds might be forthcoming for the additional work needed to support the tower. Frequent references to miracles at his shrine show that the saint was popularly adored long before his canonization in 1456. A local superstition says the tower was builded on woolpacks. According to Pliny's account, the temple of Diana of Ephesus was made firm with coats or fleeces of wool; but it is inconceivable that bags of wool were employed in either case for the foundation. At Rouen in Normandy a similar legend refers to butter as the foundation of one of the western towers, which tradition, absurd though it be, supplies the idea of a butter tax, which in turn suggests a wool tax, that in such a district as this would have been naturally a profitable source of revenue.

Probably because of the early trouble with the foundation of the great tower, there was from the first no intention of making it a belfry. Even before the spire was decided upon, the oscillation of a mass of swaying bells was obviously too dangerous to be seriously considered. A special campanile, as at Chichester, was therefore built at the north-west corner of the close. Its style was evidently similar to that of the cloisters and the chapter house. Multangular in form, an early historian calls it, but the engravings still existing show it to have been a somewhat ordinary specimen of Early English design. Its special feature was a single central pillar of Purbeck marble that supported the weight of the bells and belfry. The spire was doubtless of wood, and, [25] apparently, the upper lantern-like tower also. [6] Although its destruction is not ordered in the official document wherein the Chapter gave Wyatt authority to do so much mischief, on some pretext, probably his craze for what he called "vistas," it was demolished in the terrible destruction of 1789, opening up a view of the Cathedral that was entirely unnecessary, and wilfully destroying a feature of the close that could ill be spared.

The custom of climbing the spire during the Whitsun fair, to which Francis Price, in a naïve description, attributes much damage to the leadwork of the roofs, has only ceased in recent times, some sixty or seventy years ago. Arnold, a watchmaker, wound up his watch while leaning actually against the vane. When a lad, during a royal visit, stood on his head on the capstone, George III. refused to reward him, saying that he was bound to provide for the lives of his people. On June 26th, 1741, the timber braces of the spire were found to be on fire. According to Francis Price, "there was, about ten o'clock the night before in a very great storm, a particular flash of lightning observed by many of the inhabitants to strike against the tower with a sort of smacking noise, and then to have been lost.... It may well be called dreadful since, had it continued half an hour longer, all the assistance on earth could not have prevented the total destruction of the pile."

The West Front of the Cathedral was, beyond doubt, the last portion of the original design to be carried out, for among its details the ball-flower, a typical feature of the decorated style, frequently occurs. The governing idea of its façade is indefensible. Not merely because in common with Wells, Lincoln, and other churches, it does not emphasize the construction of the nave and aisles, and hides them by a screen, but because the screen itself poses as an integral part of the building. Even considered solely as an architectural composition, without regard to the building it professes to decorate rather than hide, it is hardly good. The two western towers it unites are, in themselves, not sufficiently important in comparison with the rest of the edifice; in fact, they are little more than finials to the screen. In many similar structures the unity of effect gained at the expense of theoretical consistency justifies the departure; here it is merely a huge surface adapted to display a great number of statues. Rich as it appears now that its long empty niches are again repeopled, it is of no remarkable [26] excellence either in mass or in detail. Its worst fault, however, is that unlike Exeter, it does not content itself by frankly assuming to be nothing more than a screen, but at first sight appears to be the legitimate finish of the nave and aisles. A recent critic, defending the façade in spite of its architectural isolation from the building in its rear, points out that the chief objection to the west front is that it is wanting in that repose and refinement of detail which characterize the rest of the building, and that its design is entirely out of keeping therewith, and also complains that "the ragged outline at the angles produced by the high relief and rather clumsy sections of the decorative detail has a very bad effect." It has been suggested that as from the position of the site there was never a chance of the building being seen from a distance — owing to the level country around it, the projection of the transepts and the group of the whole pile could never tell out as they would had it been on a hill, therefore the form chosen was deliberately adopted to give a factitious importance to the west front on its own merits. The continental builders with much more lofty nave and aisles, and with their habit of making the west door the principal entrance, were able, by enriching its portal and decorating the natural divisions of the building, to attain a stately form that honestly fulfilled its purpose; here the magnificence is secured by masking the low aisles of the nave with a wall that is a mere theatrical adjunct, its simulated windows and its stringcourses marking stories that do not exist. Apart from theoretical criticism, it is not quite admirable in itself; the three doorways are hardly of sufficient importance, the central window is somewhat larger than it should be to accord with the scale of the whole façade, while the apparently built up windows above the genuine windows of the nave aisles, whose roofs have their apex about on a level with the sills of the large central lancets, are as much frauds as any of those sham windows in symmetrical Renaissance work, which so excite the ire of ardent champions of Gothic purity.

It consists of five bays, of which the lateral ones are square turrets, covered with arcades, and terminated by spires. The lower story of the central bay is composed of three pedimented porches deeply recessed, each with a niche in its gable. Above these is a story of canopied trefoiled arches, with quatrefoil lozenges in their centres. Over this arcade is the large west window, a triplet of lancets with slender shafts and chevron ornament. Above this again is a band of quatrefoils at the foot of the gable, which is filled with double couplets of lancets with quatrefoils above their heads; and in the upper spandrils is a quatrefoiled aureole. The buttresses flanking this central bay have similar arcading continued around them. The side bays each have a triple porch, a two-lighted window with a quatrefoil in the head, with a window of the same form above it, and higher still the arcading continued from the towers.

[27]

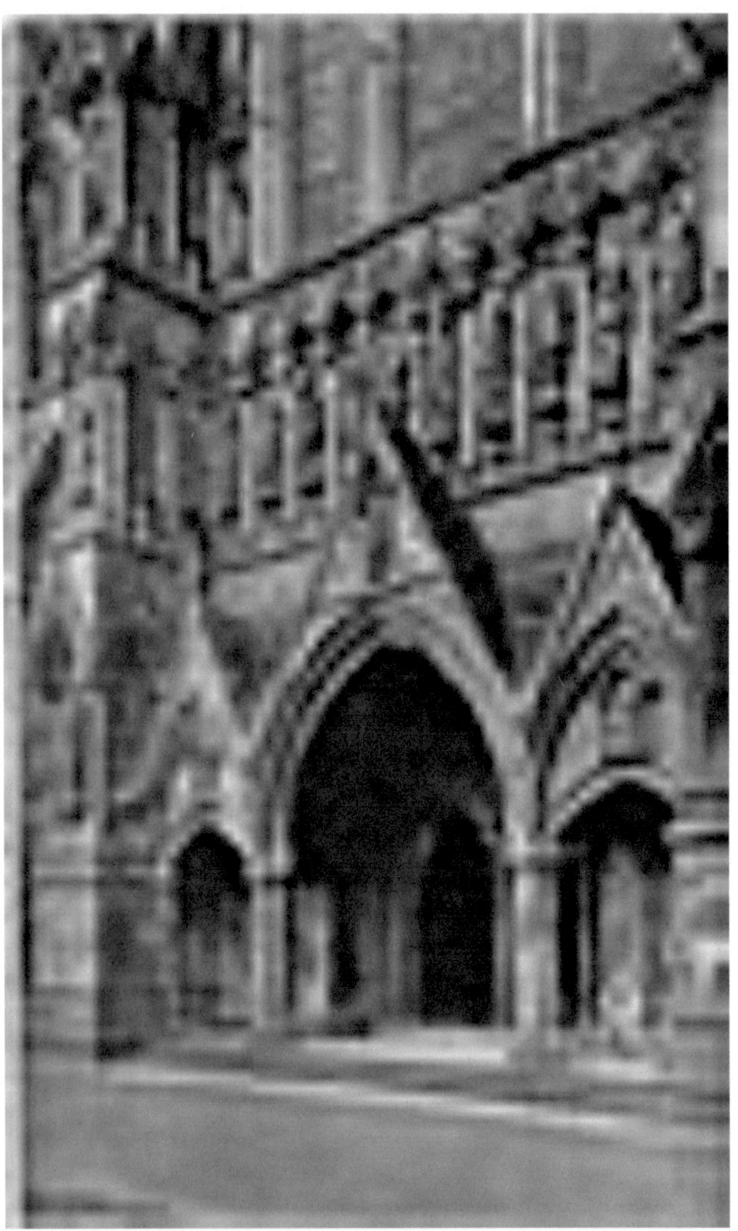

PORTALS OF THE WEST FRONT.
From a Photograph by S.B. Bolas and Co. ToList
[28]

[29] In 1863 the hundred and odd niches designed to contain statues were either despoiled or had never been occupied, with the
exception of eight which held figures mutilated beyond certain
recognition. Mr. Cockerell conjectured that two on the buttress of
the south tower represented St. Peter and St. John the Baptist, on
that to the north St. Paul and St. John the Evangelist, while a figure
facing north on the same buttress he believed to represent Stephen
Langton, Archbishop of Canterbury. Other figures are supposed to
commemorate Bishop Poore, William Longespée, 1st Earl of Salisbury, St. Stephen, and Bishop Giles de Bridport.

A sketch by Hollar, dating from the beginning of the seventeenth
century, shows the niches completely filled; and Hatcher claims
from this evidence that we are warranted in assuming that the figures were destroyed by Ludlow's troopers when he garrisoned the
belfry. But such an assumption requires many facts to support it
which are not forthcoming. We have no proof that Hollar's sketch
was intended to be a literal transcript of what he saw; it is quite
possible that for the sake of effect he preferred to complete the design according to the supposed intention of its builders. We are not
certain that the niches were all filled originally; it is quite possible
that some were purposely left vacant for future benefactors. We
know also that during the Civil War the whole fabric of the Cathedral escaped serious injuries. The Hyde family, powerful at that
time, had friends on both sides, and we find record of certain arti-
cles sent up to Parliament by one of Waller's officers were ordered
to be restored. On the other hand, the Visitation of Cathedrals, ordered and undertaken during the reign of Edward VI., had especial
instructions to remove images. In addition to these objections to
attributing the destruction of the figures to the Ludlow [30] soldiers,
there is also to be considered the natural decay of carving exposed
to the open air, which might reasonably account for the dilapidation
of a certain number.

However, whether wantonly destroyed or not, it is certain that the present figures must be all regarded as modern, since the eight actually left have been, with the exception of St. John the Baptist, very much restored. Redfern, the well-known sculptor, is responsible for the present statues. If not possessing the vigour of the old work, which from fragments in other parts of the building was certainly superior to these modern additions, yet they are creditable in design and scholarly in treatment.

The arrangement is probably in harmony with the original scheme. It represents the orders of terrestrial and celestial beings mentioned in the four verses of the hymn, "Te Deum Laudamus." In "The Legend of Christian Art," by the Rev. H.T. Armfield, Minor Canon of Salisbury (published in 1869), the symbolism and history of the whole design is given at great length. Here it must suffice to quote a few of the more salient points.

The statues are arranged in five horizontal lines from north to south, exclusive of the figure in the "vesica," the oval above. In the principal niches of the top row is a tier of angels, below this a tier of Old Testament patriarchs and prophets, then a tier of doctors, virgins, and martyrs, and lowest of all a tier of worthies, including princes, martyrs, bishops, and founders connected with the diocese and the Cathedral.

The Vesica contains a figure of our Lord seated, known technically as a "Majesty." In the tier of angels below, noting them from left to right, are the celestial hierarchies, Seraphim, Cherubim, and Thrones; Dominions, Powers, and Authorities; Principalities, Archangels, Angels. The Old Testament prophets are: David with the harp, Moses with the Tables of the Law, Abraham with the knife, Noah with the ark, Samuel with a sceptre, and Solomon with a church. The eight vacant niches should contain figures of Isaiah, Ezekiel, Elijah, Melchizedek, Enoch, Job, Daniel, and Jeremiah. The tier with the Apostles observes this order: On the northern turret St. Jude with a halberd, St. Simon Zelotes with a saw, St. Andrew with the cross that bears his name, St. Thomas with a builder's square; on the north buttress St. Peter with the keys; on the [31] southern buttress St. Paul with a sword (both these are restorations of ancient figures); on the southern turret St. James the Less with a club, St.

James the Greater with a pilgrim's staff, St. Bartholomew with the knife of his martyrdom and St. Matthias with a lance.

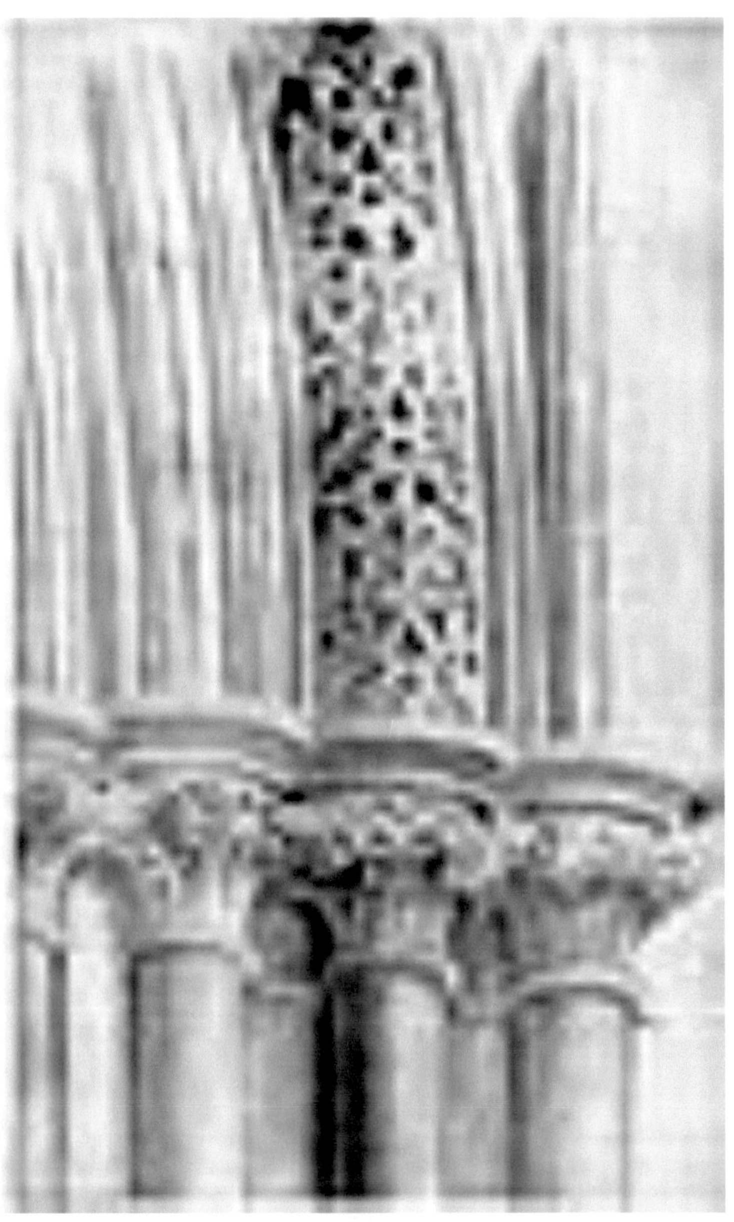

DETAILS OF MAIN WEST PORTAL.
From a Drawing by H.P. Clifford. ToList

The tier of the doctors, virgins, and martyrs, keeping to the same order, shows: St. Ambrose, Bishop of Milan, with a scourge in his right hand, and a bishop's staff in his left; St. Jerome in a cardinal's hat, with a church in his right hand and a bible in his left; St. Gregory in papal tiara, the legendary club on his shield, his pastoral staff doubly crossed, and a book, typical of his writings, on his left. On the smaller north buttress, near the turret, is a restored figure removed from its original place, which represents St. Augustine, wearing a bishop's mitre, and holding his hand as in the act of benediction. On the greater north buttress is the figure of St. Mary the Virgin, to whom the church is dedicated. This figure is also restored. In the eleven niches over the central door are, with their various symbols: St. Barbara, St. Catherine, St. Roche, St. Nicholas, St. George of England, St. Christopher, St. Sebastian, St. Cosmo, St. Damian, St. Margaret, and St. Ursula. On the greater south buttress is St. John the Baptist, and on the lesser an old figure unrestored, supposed to represent St. Bridget. On the southern turret are St. Mary, St. Agatha, St. Agnes and St. Cecilia, each wearing the martyr's crown. The tier of worthies comprises: Bishops Giles de Bridport and Richard Poore, and King Henry III. as a founder. Bishop Odo, with a wafer in his hand, commemorating the legend of his miraculous proof of the transubstantiation of the Blessed Sacrament; St. Osmund, Bishop Brithwold, St. Alban, St. Alphege, St. Edmund, and St. Thomas of Canterbury.

Another figure on the north side of the north-west turret, for some time assumed to be St. Christopher, is now assigned to St. Birinus, or possibly with more truth to St. Nicholas, who had an altar dedicated to him, "probably just at the back of this spot."

On the apex of the west front is an ancient carving of a bird on a scroll, which has puzzled many specialists. Mr. Armfield believes it to be intended for a dove, the emblem of the Holy Spirit, in a scroll to typify The Word, and thus [32] with the "Majesty" near, to be a representation of the three persons of the Trinity, in a mode in accordance with English taste.

The North Porch is a massive structure of two stories. The upper, now used as the dean's muniment room, has, like a similar example at Christchurch, Hants, no certain indication of its original use. Whether it was a dwelling for sacristans, a school, or a library, was doubtful; but later opinion thinks it was unquestionably used by the sacristans, since it is said that "the sub-treasurer of Sarum, who was usually one of the vicars choral, pledged himself to see that the clerks told off for given duties slept in the church in their accustomed places; and for himself he promised that unless lawfully excused, he would sleep each night in the treasury." Against this theory, however, it might be urged that the muniment room at the angle of the south-east transept is identified as the ancient treasury.

This porch, sometimes called the Galilee, was possibly a place where penitents met, and from which they were expelled from the church on Ash-Wednesday until Maundy Thursday. Externally, although of exquisite proportions, it has no very important details, yet its pinnacles deserve notice; but the interior is very beautiful, the walls have sunk panelling, a base arcade of foliated arches, and in the upper tier large foliated circles with sub-arches, each comprising two trefoiled arches with quatrefoil heads. Mr. G.E. Street, who thoroughly appreciated this particular period of English Gothic as his work at the New Law Courts proves, just before his death restored this part of the cathedral admirably.

Another porch, formerly the entrance to the north transept, removed by Wyatt for the most trivial reason, is now in the grounds of the college which occupies the site of the secular buildings belonging to the church of St. Edmund, founded in 1268.

The Exterior of the **Nave** is simple, but with excellently disposed features. The triple lancets of the clerestory occur in pairs between flying buttresses with tall finials; below these, in the aisles, are two two-light windows, divided by lesser buttresses terminating in gables.

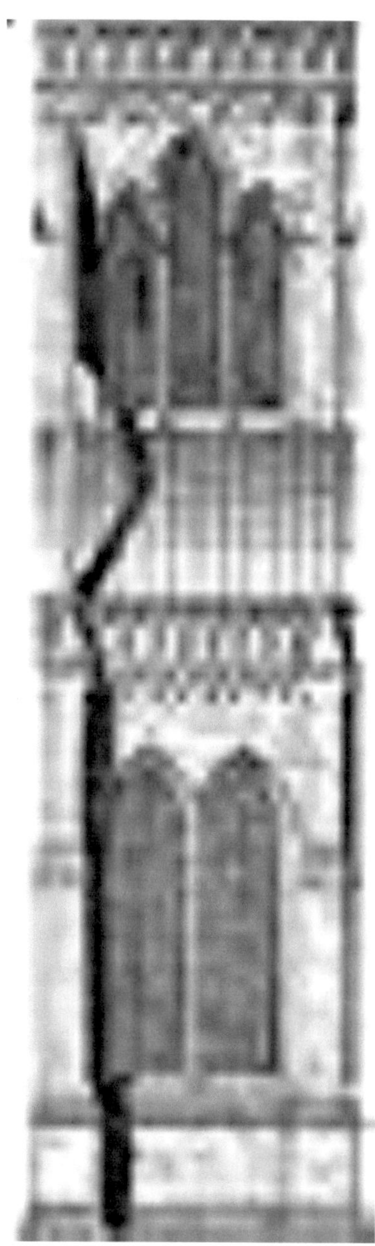

ONE BAY OF THE NAVE (EXTERIOR),
NORTH SIDE. ToList

The fronts of the main transepts show four stories, the two lower being divided into three bays by buttresses, and flanked [33] by pinnacled buttresses at each side. The doors that had a ritual use have long since been walled up both on the north and south sides. A triplet window is in the lower stage, three-light windows with quatrefoil heads occupying the second, while the third has an arcade of six lancets below a floriated circle flanked by sunk panels and quatrefoils. The windows in the gable consist of two lesser windows, two-light, with quatrefoil heads, beneath a large octofoil, the whole grouped with blank panels at the side, beneath a cinquefoil moulding. The aisle has flying buttresses reaching to the clerestory, and good angle-pinnacles. The choir transept has no dividing buttresses, and a different grouping of windows. In the lower stage is a triple lancet; there is a group of three two-light windows in the story above, and in the upper one an arcade of four lancets grouped under a comprising arch with a quatrefoil in the head. The gable is lighted by a triplet window flanked with blind lancets, and terminates in a cross.

The transepts differ slightly in detail on their north and south fronts. It has also been pointed out that while in the one transept the lancet form rules, in the other the free employment of the circle and the quatrefoil almost foreshadows the Early Decorated [34] style. The windows of both are so singularly pure in design and beautiful in proportion, that they have often been selected as typical examples of the best work in their style.

The east front of the choir is flanked with square pinnacled buttresses. Above the Lady Chapel is an arcade with five members pierced with three windows, and in the gable a similar arrangement of five lancets, three being windows, arranged in harmony with the triangular space it fills. The flying buttresses on the south side were added by Bishop Beauchamp in 1450-58.

The east front of the Lady Chapel is divided by buttresses into three bays, and has crocketed gables to each. The aisles show a lancet in the lower story, with a blind couplet beneath a quatrefoil in the gable; the central compartment has a triplet in each story.

The south side corresponds in character to the north, but is partly hidden by the chapter house, the muniment room, the library, and cloisters. The walls of the latter are high, and the quadrangle they inclose entirely separated from the building, the long narrow space between being known as the Plumbery.

Many consecration crosses of beautiful design are to be found on the building marking the spots touched by the oil of unction at the dedication of the edifice. (See initial letter, page 1.)

The cathedral is built of freestone from the Chilmark quarries twelve miles distant, with a lavish use of Purbeck marble in its interior. The grey colour of the leaden roofs and the pure unstained tone of its walls, impart a quasi-modern aspect to it, which, no matter how little justified by facts, always presents Salisbury to one's mind, as a late addition to the superb array of English churches; yet considering that as we see it from the Close no portion (except possibly the spire) later than the twelfth century comes into the picture, there is no other cathedral that so little justifies such an impression, and one cannot escape a return to the first reason advanced, namely, that its singular unity has given it an aspect of perpetual youth. [35]

[36]

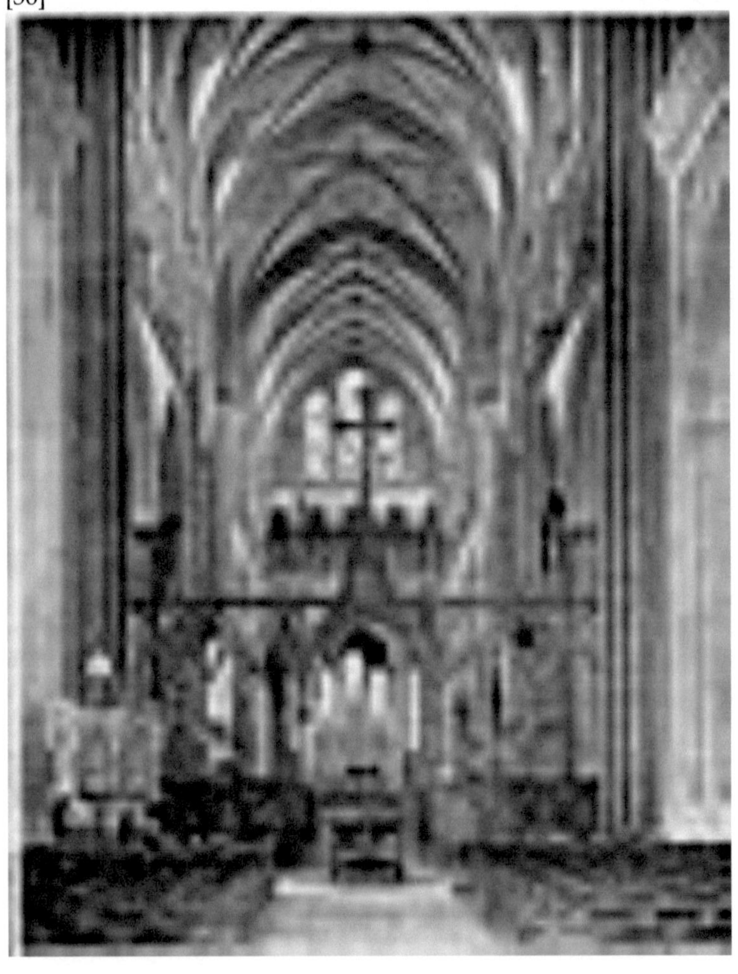

THE CHOIR SCREEN.
From a Photograph by Carl Norman and Co. ToList

FOOTNOTES:

[4] This was carefully replaced in its original position inclosed in a copper cylinder.

[5] Recently, however, anxiety has been again aroused, and the spire has been once more strengthened.

[6] This lantern story was removed in 1757 by order of the Dean and Chapter.

[37]

THE INTERIOR OF THE CATHEDRAL AND CHAPTER HOUSE.

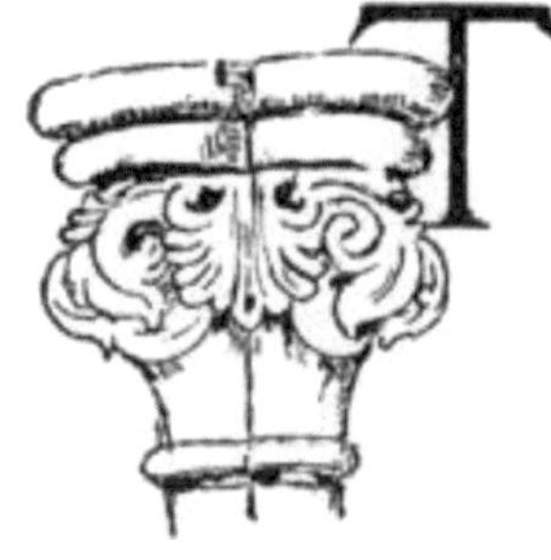

The ground plan of Salisbury is a well-proportioned double cross with the arms, of the choir transepts, more important than usual. Indeed, the exquisitely proportioned and balanced symmetry of every portion, as of the whole, which almost places Salisbury among classic buildings, is as marked in its ground plan as in any part of the building. As an appreciative student of the building has written: "This is the great beauty of Salisbury, the composition of its mighty body as a whole. So finely proportioned and arranged are its square masses of different heights and sizes, so splendid are the broad effects of light and shadow they produce, so appropriate is the slant of the roof lines, and so nicely placed and gracefully shaped are the simple windows, that for once we can give no thought of regret either to the circling apses of continental lands or the rich traceries and surface carvings and figures—sculptures of later generations. The whole effect is in the strictest sense architectural. Few large buildings teach so clearly the great lesson that beauty in a building depends first of all upon composition, not decoration; upon masses, not details; upon the use and shaping, not the ornamentation of features; and very few show half so plainly that mediæval architects could realize this fact. We are too apt to think that Gothic art cannot be individual without being eccentric, or interesting without being heterogeneous ... but Salisbury is both grand and lovely, and yet it is [38] quiet, rational, and all of a piece, clear and smooth, and refined to the point of utmost purity. No building in the world is more logical, more lucid in expression, more restful to the mind and eye." [7]

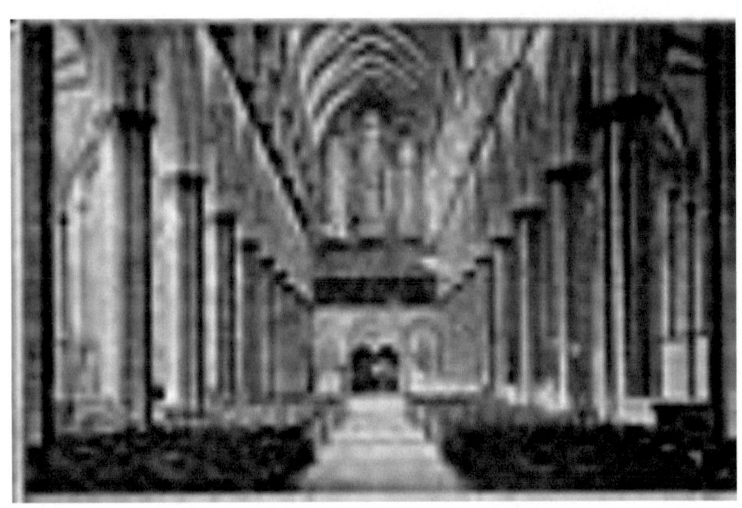

THE NAVE, LOOKING WEST.
From a Photograph by Messrs. Poulton. ToList

The number of its pillars, windows, and doorways is said to equal the hours, days, and months of the year; hence the local rhyme, attributed, on the authority of Godwin, to a certain Daniel Rogers:

> "As many days as in one year there be,
> So many windows in this church we see;
> As many marble pillars here appear
> As there are hours throughout the fleeting year;
> As many gates as moons one year does view —
> Strange tale to tell! yet not more strange than true."

Fuller, speaking of these, by a curious lapse falls into the vulgar error of believing Purbeck marble to be an artificial product [39] melted and poured into moulds, says: "The cathedral is paramount of its kind, wherein the doors and chapels equal the months, the windows the days, the pillars and pillarets of fusile marble (an ancient art now shrewdly suspected to be lost) the hours of the year; so that all Europe affords not such an almanac of architecture. Once walking in this church (whereof then I was prebendary) I met a countryman wondering at the structure thereof. 'I once,' said he to me, 'admired that there could be a church that should have so many pillars as there be hours in the year, and now I admire more, that there should be so many hours in the year as I see pillars in this church.'"

The Nave. — The first glimpse as we enter by the west door is undoubtedly impressive, notwithstanding the absence of colour and the lack of mystery for which the complete vista obtained at such a cruel cost by Wyatt is insufficient compensation. The whole scheme of decoration in its pristine state must have been extremely beautiful. "If you can imagine it with the walls and piers exhibiting strong contrasts of colour in the dark and polished Purbeck shafts and the lighter freestones, the arches picked out with colours, the groining elaborately decorated, and the whole lighted by brilliantly painted windows with a preponderance of dark blue and ruby, together with a flood of white light showing through the lancet of the centre, we may be allowed a doubt whether Tintern or York could have compared with it." Add to this picture the movable hangings and decorations of its many altars, and we cannot honestly attribute the coldness of the present effect to any fault in the original design. Elsewhere this austerity of monochrome is modified to a great extent by the variety (anachronisms though they be) of later architectural insertions. Salisbury, through the very purity of its design, especially suffers from its translation from chromatic harmony to monotone, for although possibly the architectural details are thereby rendered more apparent, yet the exaggeration of what is after all but the skeleton of the building, destroys the effect of the whole as its architect imagined it.

Clustered columns of unpolished Purbeck marble on a quatrefoil plan, with smaller detached shafts of lustrous marble at the cardinal points, support, on either side, the ten great arches of the first story of the nave. These polished shafts are [40] generally in two pieces, with a brass ring covering the joint; Francis Price discusses, at great length, this constant feature of the whole building, and points out, that although most of the shafts were probably not in place until after the masonry was fairly set, yet frequently subsequent settlement has crushed them; although, in the nave, the main piers in small blocks laid according to the natural bed of the stone, are still perfectly sound. The large arches are gracefully moulded with masses of carved foliage at the intersections.

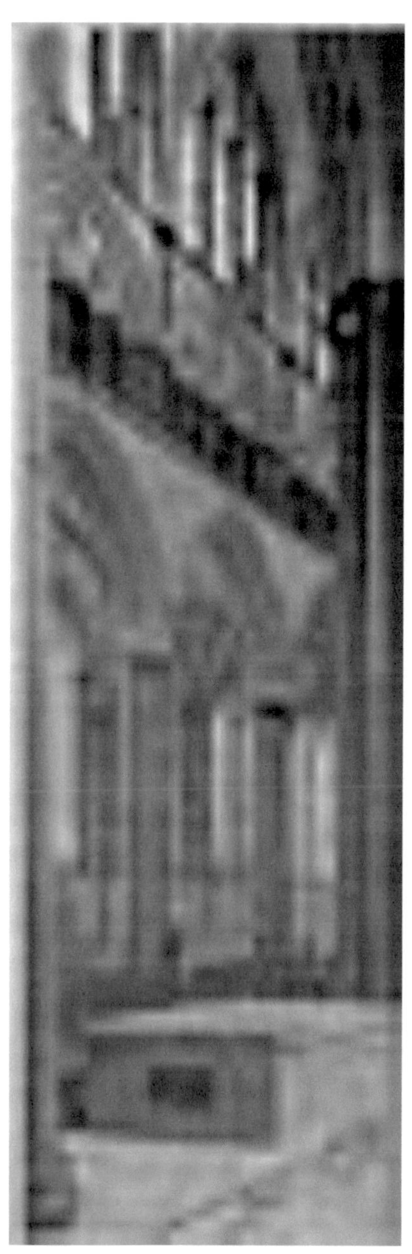

THE NAVE—SOUTH SIDE. ToList

In the nave of this cathedral we have a very uncommon feature in the connected base of the main columns, which was doubtless introduced to aid in distributing the weight over a larger surface, and so to overcome the treacherous character of the foundation.

The triforium, which, from its style, naturally suggests comparison with Westminster, and the Angel Choir of Lincoln, is simple, but extremely beautiful. Each of its rather flat-pointed arches, equalling in span that of the main arch below, is subdivided into pairs, which again each inclose two smaller ones. These are decorated with trefoils and quatrefoils, alternately with [41] cinquefoils and octofoils. Immediately above the carving, at the intersection of the main arches, is a corbelled head, from which rises a triple vaulting-shaft with foliated capitals, on a line with the base of the clerestory. This upper story has, in each bay of the vaulting, simple lancet windows grouped in threes. The arches here, as in almost every instance throughout the building, are supported by Purbeck marble shafts. The nave aisles are lighted by double lancet-windows in each bay. The most noticeable feature of these aisles is the stone bench which extends the whole length of the building on both the north and south sides.

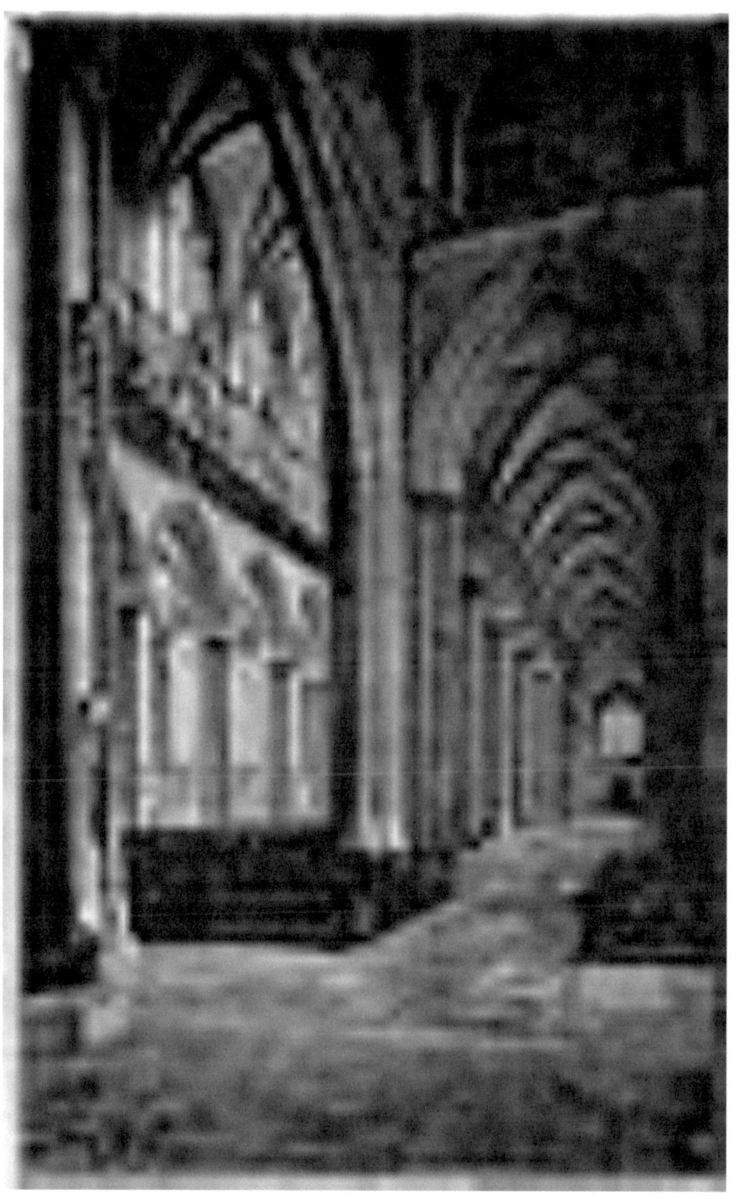

The west wall is panelled in three main arches, with an upper story reaching to the height of the triforium base, and containing an arcade of four arches, subdivided each into two smaller trefoiled ones, with cinquefoil heads. Above these is the triplet lancet of the great west window. The effect of the nave looking west is clearly shown in the photograph here reproduced.

Of the chapels and altars once existing we have records in various documents. In the "Sarum Processional" twelve altars are mentioned, dedicated respectively to SS. Andrew, Nicholas, John the Baptist, Margaret, Mary Magdalene, Laurence, Michael, Martin, Catherine, Edward, Edmund the King, and Edmund, Archbishop of Canterbury. The sites of these so far as they can be traced appears to have been: St. [42] Catherine and St. Martin in the north choir transept, St. Nicholas and St. Mary Magdalene in the south, and St. Edmund of Canterbury and St. Margaret respectively in the north and south great transepts.

Throughout the nave it is evident that the first plans were rigidly obeyed, although the severity of the early years of the style had become much modified before the work was finished. The absence of ornate decoration, the simplicity of the mouldings, and the plate-tracery of the triforium all indicate the first period of "Early English."

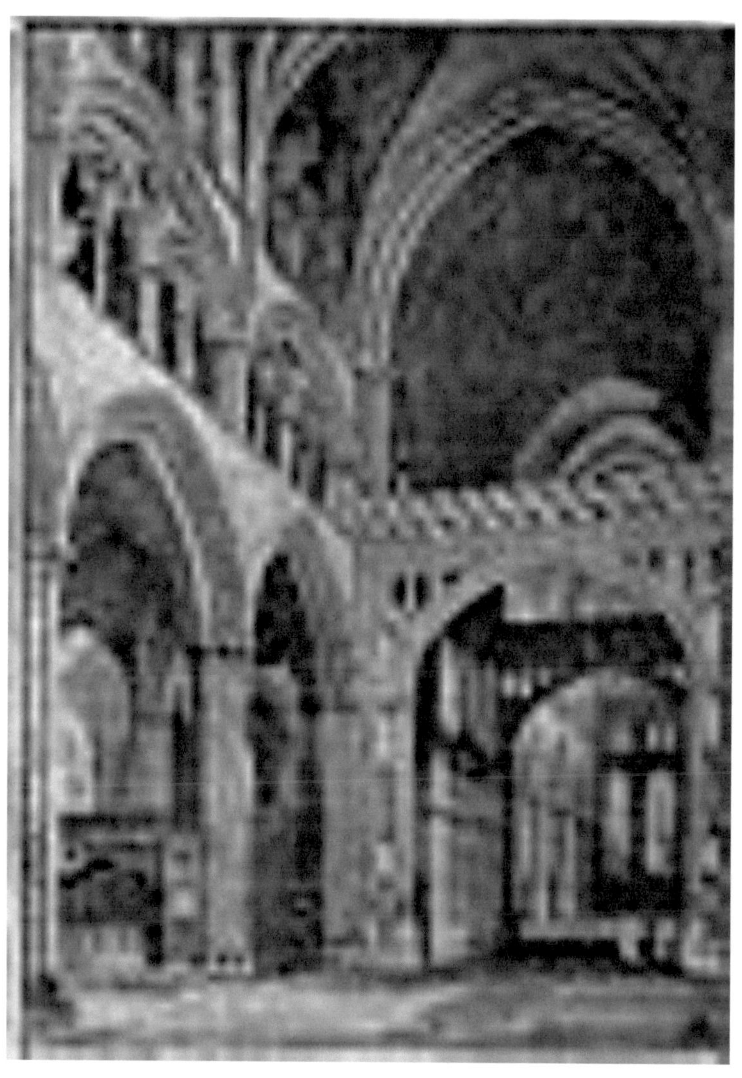

NAVE TRANSEPT. ToList

The dimensions of the nave are: 229 feet 6 inches long, 82 feet wide, and 81 feet high. The aisles are 17 feet 6 inches wide, and 39 feet 9 inches high.

The Nave Transepts are in three stories, with eastern [43] aisles divided into three bays. The screens inclosing chapels in these were demolished by Wyatt. Above the entrances to the great transepts are arches inserted by Bishop Beauchamp (1450-1481) to withstand the side thrust of the great tower. These are of perpendicular work, with their spandrils panelled and their cornices battlemented, as shown in the engraving. Canterbury and Wells, in a far more prominent fashion, have similar features; in this instance the addition appears to have succeeded in its purpose to insure the stability of the tower. In the choir transepts these additional features take the form of an inverted arch, above the main arch. The vaulting of the tower roof is also in the perpendicular style and shows excellent groined work. Both Sir Christopher Wren and Francis Price, call its four main pillars the legs of the tower.

Of the transept Fuller says: "The cross aisle of this church is the most beautiful and lightsome of any I have yet beheld. The spire steeple (not founded on the ground, but for the main supported by four pillars,) is of great height and greater workmanship. I have been credibly informed that some foreign artists beholding this building brake forth into tears, which some imputed to their admiration (though I see not how wondering could cause weeping): others to their envy, grieving that they had not the like in their own land."

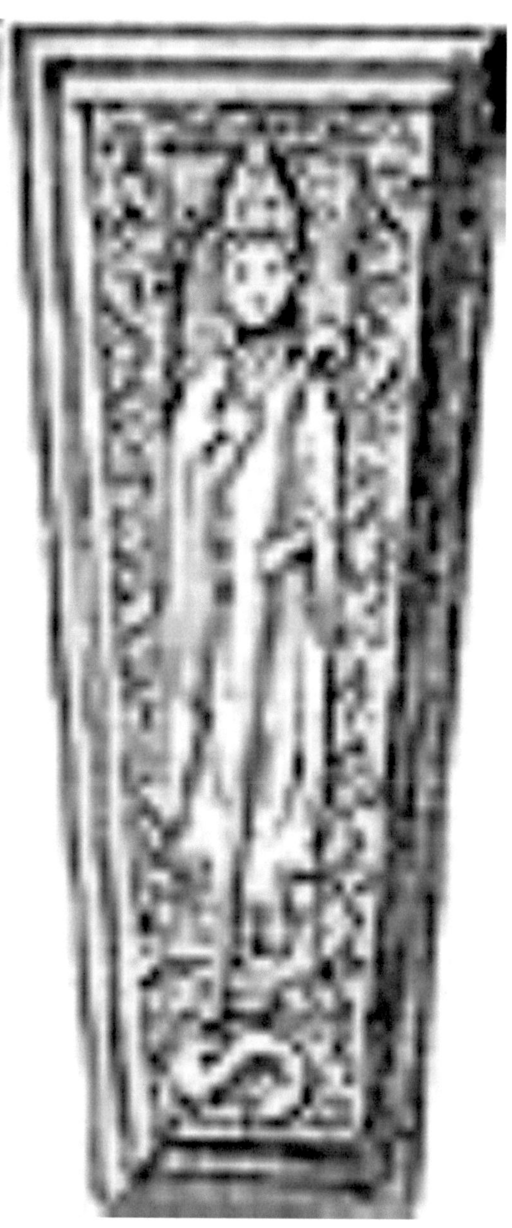

ToList

Monuments in the Nave. [8] — The peculiar arrangements of the ancient monuments in two long rows on the continuous plinth that connects the bases of the pillars on each side of the nave is another of Wyatt's freaks during his terrible innovations in 1789. Not only did he sever the historical associations of centuries by these arbitrary removals, but paid so little attention to consistency that portions of monuments belonging to entirely different periods were combined with curious results, and remains transferred to other "receptacles" than those designed for them. It is true that the effect of the present arrangement is not entirely bad, but it was not worth achieving at such a cost.

The first monument on the south side as we enter by the great west door, is in memory of Thomas Lord Wyndham of Finglass, Lord Chancellor of Ireland, (1) who died in 1745; the marble figure of Hibernia which surmounts it is by [44] Rysbrack. At the western base of the first south pillar is a Purbeck marble slab, (2) coffin-shaped, probably the oldest monument in the building. This is usually assigned to Bishop Herman, whose tomb it is supposed to have covered in Old Sarum; but no evidence exists to support this theory. In the first place his original burial-place is entirely unknown, and William de Wanda, who chronicles minutely the removal of the bodies of other bishops from the old cathedral, does not even mention Herman's name.

The next (3) is an effigy of a bishop in full pontificals, also believed to have been originally at Old Sarum. The carving is rich, and the design a fine example of the early Norman style. The chasuble is decorated with stars, and the dalmatic has a rich border. Elaborately carved foliage, with birds, frames the figure, which has its right hand raised in the attitude of benediction, and grasps a pastoral staff in the left. It is usually believed that it commemorates Bishop Jocelin, who died in 1184, and was probably removed from Old Sarum at the translation of the bodies of the three bishops. The head of the effigy is evidently a much later restoration, probably, from the style of the richly ornamented mitre, about the time of Henry III. or Edward I. As the face is cleanly shaven, while the seal of Bishop Jocelin depicts him as bearded, some antiquaries hold this monument to belong to Bishop Roger, and assign to Bishop Jocelin the one formerly attributed to Bishop Herman. If, however, differences of opinion exist concerning the identity of these two effigies, they are as nothing compared to the uncertainty regarding the next, (4) which represents a bishop holding a pastoral staff. Down the front of this cope are the words, "Affer opem devenies in idem." Hatcher and Duke believe that it represents Bishop Jocelin. Britton, Gough and Planché, prefer to think that it commemorates Bishop Roger. Its inscription on the edge of the slab runs:

> "Flent hodie Salesberie quia decidit ensis
> Justitie, pater ecclesiæ Salisberiensis
> Dum viguit, miseros aluit, fastusque potentum
> [45] Non timuit, sed clava fuit terrorque nocentum
> De Ducibus, de nobilibus primordia duxit
> Principibus, propeque tibi gemma reluxit."

A version given in the Wilts Archeo. Mag. vol. xvii. runs: "They mourn to-day at Salesberie because there has fallen the sword of justice, the Father of the Church of Salesberie. While he lived he sustained the oppressed and wretched, and feared not the arrogance of the powerful, but himself was the scourge (literally, the club) and terror of the guilty. He traced his ancestry from dukes and noble princes, who shone near thee as a precious gem." Another item of indirect evidence supplied by this inscription is worth noting, namely, the "l" in Salisberie. The period when this letter superseded the "r" was about the time of Jocelin's death. Only a single coin of Stephen's has the "l."

To Bishop Roger reference is made on page 100, and it is evident that even the fulsome praise of an epitaph would hardly go out of its way to describe him as "sprung from dukes and noble princes." Planché, despite this objection, does not deem it convincing, as poor priests were often of noble lineage. If, however, we assume it represents Bishop Jocelin, one of the house of Bohun, a great Norman family, and compare the effigy with the seal of that bishop, the later theory that deprives Bishop Roger of this much discussed monument will probably be chosen as the most acceptable. In a record at least three centuries old his burial-place is said to be near the chapel of St. Stephen; and in a plan of the Cathedral, dated 1773, and in Price's account, 1774, a plain slab with a cross upon it, in a shallow recess of the wall east of the north aisle, is assigned to Bishop Roger.

But this and the other disputed monuments are undoubtedly genuine memorials of the earliest bishops, and not merely interesting for that reason, but as (with the exception of two slabs dated 1086 and 1172 in Westminster Abbey) the earliest examples of their class in England. Although the question of their identity of the individuals they commemorate were best left to those few who are peculiarly concerned with the history of the period that includes them.

Near these effigies is a slab with faint traces of an incised figure, which may possibly have represented an abbot or prior. It can hardly be intended for a bishop, as no mitre can be [46] traced, and the staff is held in the right hand. The monument (5) on the plinth under the next arch is also beyond identification.

Next in order comes the altar tomb (6) which now contains the remains of Bishop Beauchamp, who died in 1481. When this was removed from the aisle at the north end of the great transept it was empty, and showed no trace of its original dedication. During the wanton demolition of the Beauchamp chantry, where, "in marble tumbes," with his father and mother on either hand, the remains of Bishop Beauchamp had been unmolested for over three hundred years, his own tomb was "mislaid" and never recovered. It is pleasant to note that even the apologists for Wyatt felt this incident was beyond their sympathy. Dodsworth naïvely remarks, "After this the greatest possible care was taken that nothing of the kind should again occur," and so far as we know, not even a prior was subsequently lost. Of this bishop much is said elsewhere in this book, and his beautiful chantry described on page 90.

The elaborate effigy (7) beneath the next arch represents Robert Lord Hungerford clad in a superb suit of fifteenth century plate armour, with the collar of SS. round his neck, and with "his hair polled" in the fashion of Henry V. A superbly decorated sword and dagger hang from his jewelled girdle at his side, while his feet rest upon a dog wearing a rich collar. This monument was placed originally between the Lady Chapel and the (Hungerford) chantry founded by Margaret, his widow. By his will Lord Hungerford directed that his body should be interred before the altar of St. Osmund. The tomb beneath the effigy is made up from portions of the chapel.

The monument known as Lord Stourton's (8), removed from the east end of the Cathedral, is next in order. Its three apertures on each side are said to be emblematic of the six sources of the river Stour, which rises at Storrhead, the ancient family seat, from whence the name is derived. The whole shape of the tomb is so unusual that in spite of the theory that it represents the six sources of the Stour, the curious arched openings appear as if pierced to exhibit something behind them. Yet this could not have been an effigy, for the interior is divided by a solid partition of stone. The pillars which stood between the arches are gone. Lord Stourton, to whom it is attributed, was hanged with a silken cord on March 6th, 1556, in the Salisbury market-place. The tragedy is too long to [47] give in detail, as it is told in the country histories and elsewhere, here a brief summary must suffice:—When his mother became a widow Lord Stourton attempted to induce her to sign a bond promising that she would never re-marry. The family agents, a father and son named Hartgill, sided with Lady Stourton and seemed to have influenced her in declining to assent to the scheme. The Hartgills after much physical maltreatment at the hands of Lord Stourton's mercenaries, took legal action against him, with the result that he was fined and imprisoned for awhile in the Fleet. When let out on parole he invited the Hartgills to meet him that he might pay them the fine. Upon their appearance at Kilmington Churchyard, the appointed place, they were seized by armed men, carried away and murdered in cold blood in full sight of Lord Stourton himself the same night. For this he was committed to the Tower, tried at Westminster and hanged with four of his men at Salisbury. So late as 1775 a wire twisted into a noose was suspended above his tomb.

The mutilated effigy (9) of Bishop de la Wyle (died 1271) rests on a base made up of portions of later work. The last monument on this side (10) is of the famous William Longespée, 1st Earl of Salisbury, the natural son of Henry II. by Fair Rosamond. This effigy still shows traces of the gorgeous ornament in gold and colours with which it was originally decorated. Westmacott, the sculptor, says:

"The manly, warrior character of the figure is particularly striking even in its recumbent attitude, while the turn of the head, and the graceful flow of lines in the right hand and arm, with the natural heavy fall of the chain armour at the side, exhibit a feeling of art that would not do discredit to a very advanced school." The figure is clad in mail armour, which covers the mouth in a peculiar fashion, and wears a surcoat falling in simple folds, almost Greek in feeling, that are somewhat curious in connection with the rich mediæval luxuriance of the surface ornament. On his shield are borne six heraldic leopards or lions. The slab and effigy are stone, but the base is of wood encircled by an arcade of trefoiled arches. One of its compartments protected with glass yet shows a piece of the beautiful diaper work, in silver overlaid on white linen, remains of the rich colourings of two successive periods are present on the effigy itself. (See p. 94.)

Crossing the nave, and following the northern base of the [48] pillars, we find a very beautiful alabaster monument (11), with the effigy of Sir John Cheyney (died 1509) clad in military garb, and wearing the collar of SS. with the portcullis badge of Henry VII. suspended therefrom. Sir John Cheyney was the standard-bearer of Henry of Richmond at Bosworth Field. To quote from Hall's "Chronicle" — "King Richard set on so sharply at the first brount that he ouerthrew th'erle's standard and slew Sir William Brandon, his standard-bearer, and matched hand to hand with John Cheynye, a man of great strength, who would have resisted him, and the said John was by him manfully ouerthrowen." Wyatt, in his ghoulish explorations exhumed Sir John's bones, and confirmed the legend of his gigantic stature; the thigh-bone was found to be twenty-one inches in length, four inches more than the standard average. His original tomb was destroyed with the rest of the Beauchamp chapel, and his remains now lie beneath this effigy. Under the next arch to the westward are two tombs (12,13) deprived of the brasses they once bore, which represented Walter, Lord Hungerford, and his first wife, Catherine Peverell. The famous iron chapel has been removed to the choir by their descendant, the Earl of Radnor, who converted the monument into a family pew.

The plain altar tomb of St. Osmund, that, moved hither by Wyatt, stood until 1878 below the next arch of the nave; is now replaced in the Lady Chapel on its former site.

The effigy of Sir John de Montacute (14) (died 1389) clad in mail and chain armour, is, according to Meyrick, "a good specimen of highly ornamented gauntlets, of a contrivance for the easier bending of the body at the bottom of the breastplate, and of the elegant manner of twisting the hanging sword belt, pendant from the military girdle, round the upper part of the sword." The head of the figure reposes on a helmet, a lion couches at his feet. Armorial bearings appear on shields at the sides of the tomb. (See p. 79.)

Then we come to Chancellor Geoffrey's tomb (15), and the next (16) has not been identified. The larger effigy (17) on the last portion of the northern plinth is of William Longespée, fourth Earl of Salisbury; the figure wears chain armour, and lies with its legs crossed and hands grasped upon his sword. He was twice a Crusader, in 1240-1242, and in 1249, when he served with St. Louis of France at Damietta, he fell in battle near Cairo in 1250, and was buried in the church of the [49] Holy Cross near Acre. The night he was killed, according to Matthew Paris, his mother, the Countess Ela, saw in a vision "the heavens opened, and her son armed at all points, with the six lioncels on his shield, received in triumph by a company of angels." Many strange marvels were reported to have been worked by his bones.

The Boy Bishop.—Near this monument is the one (18) known as the "Boy Bishop." Hidden for a long time underneath some seats near the pulpit, it was brought to light in 1680, and moved to its present position. At first it was covered with a wooden box; for which later on, owing to the great curiosity shown by the public, the strong iron grating which now protects it was substituted. (See p. 98.)

Notwithstanding that the ceremony of the Boy Bishop was observed at Salisbury for many centuries, there is no reasonable proof that this effigy has any connection therewith. Even John Gregory, whose famous treatise on the Boy Bishop is printed in "Gregorii Posthuma," 1649-1669, admits there that it might well seem impossible to everyone that either a bishop should be so small in person or a child so great in clothes. Thomas Fuller also echoes the same objection when he writes: "But the curiosity of critics is best entertained with the tomb in the north of the nave of the church, where lieth a monument in stone of a little boy, habited all in episcopal robes, a mitre upon his head, a crozier in his hand, and the rest accordingly. At the discovery thereof, formerly covered over with pews, many justly admired that either a bishop could be so small in person or a child so great in clothes; though since all is unriddled; for it was then fashionable in that church (a thing rather deserving to be remembered than fit to be done), in the depth of Popery, that the choristers chose a boy of their society to be a bishop among them from St. Nicholas' till Innocents' day." If the effigy represents a boy it is hard to explain why it is not life-size. Stothard in his "Monumental Effigies," in common with most later authorities, favours the idea that it is a miniature representation of a real bishop. Canon Jones suggests probably Walter Scammel, Henry de Braundeston, or William de la Corner. Mackenzie Walcott inclined to the belief that it represented Bishop Wykehampton, who died 1284. A small figure of Bishop Ethelman, 1260, about the same date, is in Winchester Cathedral; there is also one [50] 14-½ inches long in Abbey Dore Church, Herefordshire, one at Ayot, St. Lawrence, Herts, 2 feet 3 inches, and other small effigies of knights and civilians elsewhere. According to Digby Wyatt the custom of burying different portions of the body in different places was common in the twelfth and thirteenth centuries; from which he infers that probably these figures commemorated the place of sepulture of the heart.

Whether the monument in question be connected with the Chorister Bishop or not, there are so many records of the function with which popular credence has associated it, that a short digression is almost unavoidable. The pamphlet by John Gregory is elaborately minute and much too long to be quoted fully, yet some of the facts he brought together may be briefly noted. It seems that on the feast of St. Nicholas, the patron saint of children, the choir-boys [9] elected one of their number, who from that day to the feast of the Holy Innocents, December 28th, bore the rank and exercised the functions of a bishop, the other choristers being his prebendaries. During his term of office he wore episcopal vestments. On the eve of the Holy Innocents he performed the entire office, excepting the mass, as a real bishop would have done. At Salisbury on that day the boy-bishop and his boy-prebendaries went in procession to the altar of the Holy Trinity, taking precedence of the dean and resident canons. At the first chapter afterwards the boy bishop attended in person and was permitted to receive the entire Oblation made at the altar during the day of his procession. The names of many of the choristers and the amounts of the oblations offered for the boy-bishops are the subject of many entries in the capitular registers of both English and continental churches. Bishop Mortival in his statutes, still preserved among the cathedral muniments, orders that the bishop of the choristers "shall make no visit (some commentators consider this has been misinterpreted, to infer that elsewhere he held visitations), nor keep any feast, but shall remain in the Common Hall, unless he be invited to the table of a Canon for recreation." The order of service in use in this diocese has been preserved (MS. No. 153 of the Cathedral Library); in it we find as a special collect, "O [51] Almighty God, who out of the mouths of babes and sucklings," etc., not, however, quite in the form in which it appears in the Prayer Book of Ed. VI.

The spectacle was so popular, and attracted such great crowds, that by special edict it was prescribed that the penalty of the greater excommunication should be incurred by those who might interrupt or press upon the boys during their procession or in any part of their service.

In spite of the doubts thrown upon the monument at Salisbury, it is distinctly recorded that if a boy-bishop died during his term of power, he was to be buried in his vestments and have his obsequies celebrated with the pomp pertaining to an episcopal funeral.

This custom was not confined to this cathedral, but practised at many others in England and on the Continent, where we find records of much greater power being exercised by the boy-prelate, extending even to the presentation to prebends. At Winchester it was certainly observed. So far back as 1263 we find it described at St. Paul's Cathedral as an ancient custom. Several sermons preached by the boy-bishops are still preserved; one is reprinted in the Camden Society's "Miscellany," vol. vii. Dean Colet (once a prebendary of Sarum) in his statutes for St. Paul's school directs: "All these children shall every Childermas day come to Paules Church, and here the Childe-bishoppes sermon, and after be at high masse so each of them offer *one peny* to the childe bishoppe. And with the maisters and surveyors of the scoole in general procession when they be warned they shall go tweyne and tweyne togither soberly, and not singe oute, but saye devoutly tweyne by tweyne seven psalmes with letany." (Add. MS. 6174.) At York the mock prelate held office longer, and wielded far more power than his fellows of Sarum.

In 1299, on December 7th, a boy-bishop at Hoton, near Newcastle-on-Tyne, said vespers before Edward I., then on his way to Scotland.

At Salisbury in 1542 Henry VIII. forbade the ceremony by royal proclamation. It was revived under Queen Mary, and finally abolished on the accession of Queen Elizabeth.

Not entirely alien to the subject is the office of the bishop's boy, which is probably peculiar to Salisbury. His duty is to call at the palace before every service and inquire if the bishop [52] will attend. He is formally appointed by the bishop, who lays his hands upon him, and repeats a prescribed office.

A nameless tomb (19), and a memorial (20) to Dr. Daubigny Turberville, an oculist of Salisbury, who died April 21st, 1696, complete the more important monuments of the nave. Several mural tablets on the aisle walls are of hardly sufficient general interest to need description. In Price's "Antiquities of Salisbury," and many of the numerous works devoted to the cathedral, copies of nearly all the epitaphs are given, but, except in very special instances, they form peculiarly depressing reading.

The Choir Screen was given as a memorial of the late Mr. Sidney Lear by his wife, to whom the cathedral is indebted for many of its modern enrichments. It is entirely of wrought metal, by Skidmore, of Coventry, and a good example of its class. It replaced the organ screen compiled by Wyatt from fragments of the Hungerford and Beauchamp chantries; to erect which he removed the original screen of exquisite workmanship, as may be seen by portions now placed along the west wall of the north-east transept.

The Organ, that stood on the old screen until lately, was built by Green, of Isleworth, and a gift from King George III. in his capacity as "a Berkshire gentleman," that county being included in the diocese of Sarum until 1836. It was given by the Dean and Chapter to the church of St. Thomas. The present organ, a fine instrument, built by Willis, was the gift of Miss Chafyn Grove, is placed in the second arcade on each side of the choir, the necessary connecting mechanism being in a tunnel below the pavement, while the larger pipes and the bellows are inclosed within a screen in the north transept. The oak case is from a design by the late Mr. Street.

The Choir and Presbytery are very similar to the nave in the main features of their design. The piers show a different plan, which provides for eight shafts of Purbeck marble to each. The inner mouldings of the arches exhibit the "dog-tooth" ornamentation of their period. The triforium and clerestory differ slightly from the corresponding parts of the nave. In each of the last two bays of the presbytery the triforium has five small cinquefoil arches. At the east wall of the choir above the reredos is an arcade of [53] five simply-pointed arches, below a triplet window in the gable, which is filled with stained glass, given by the Earl of Radnor in 1781, and representing "The Brazen Serpent," after a design by Mortimer.

The choir still bears traces of Wyatt's destruction. He removed the original reredos behind the high altar and the screen before the Lady Chapel, so that both, with the low eastern aisle, were thrown into the choir. He shifted the high altar from the choir to the extreme east end of the Lady Chapel, sacrificing several chantries and tombs to do so. Views of the cathedral after his reign of terror fail to show any gain to compensate for so much loss; the extreme length is not apparently an advantage, while the bare look of the interior seems decidedly intensified by the increased vista that he was so delighted to obtain, and for which with a light heart he effaced the silent records of dead centuries.

The Decorations of the Roof of the choir and presbytery are reproductions by Messrs. Clayton and Bell of the original paintings, which dated probably from the thirteenth century. The series, commencing from the west, shows twenty-four prophets and saints, all, with the exception of St. John the Baptist, selected from the Old

Testament. Taking them in lines parallel with the choir screen, the first row contains (reading from the left, as one faces the altar): Zechariah, Daniel, Ezekiel, and St. John the Baptist; the second: Zacharias, Joel, Hosea, and Zephaniah; the third: Job, Habakkuk, Nahum, David; the fourth: Moses, Micah, Jonah, and Jacob; the fifth: Malachi, Obadiah, Amos, and Isaac; and the sixth: Haggai, Jeremiah, Isaiah, and Abraham. In the square of the transept crossing are (following the same order): St. Thomas and St. Andrew, St. Matthew and St. John, St. Philip and St. Simon, St. Bartholomew and St. Matthias. At the left the last panel on that side contains St. Peter and St. Andrew, while another in the opposite corner has St. James and St. John. In the centre is a figure of Christ, in majesty, surrounded by the four evangelists.

From this point to the east the panels are devoted to secular subjects typifying the twelve months, "The signs of the Zodiac," Price calls them: January, warming at a fire; February, drinking wine; March, delving; April, sowing; May, hawking; June, flowers; July, reaping; August, threshing; September, fruit; [54] October, brewing; November, cutting wood; December, killing the fatted pig. The originals were white, or rather buff-washed, in the last century. Owing to the tenacity of this wash, and the friable non-adhesive quality of the paint it covered, it was found impossible to remove the additional coating without destroying the original paintings. Tracings of some of them were made by Messrs. Clayton and Bell; but although the semi-transparent character of the buff wash allowed the subjects to be discerned from below; on nearer inspection the details became blurred and shapeless.

The theory that the paintings of the choir had been re-painted before their defacement by buff wash seems hardly likely from the state reported by the restorers. The idea probably arose from an extract, itself possibly interpolated, frequently quoted from one edition of Defoe's "Tour through the Island of Great Britain:" "The choir resembles a theatre rather than a venerable choir of a church; it is painted white with the panels golden, and groups and garlands of roses and other flowers intertwined run round the top of the stalls; each stall hath the arms of its holder in gilt letters or blue writ on it; and the episcopal throne with Bishop Ward's arms upon it would make a fine theatrical decoration, being supported by gilt pillars and painted with flowers upon white all over. The roof of the choir hath some fresh painting, containing several saints as big as life, each in a circle by itself and holding a label in their hands telling who they are. The altar piece is very mean, and behind this altar, in the Virgin Mary's Chapel, are some very good monuments." But in the first edition of the same book Defoe himself says: "The inside is certainly hurt by the paltry old paintings in and over the choir, and the whitewashing badly done, wherein they have very stupidly everywhere drawn black lines to imitate joints of stone." In another edition of 1724 the passage reads: "The painting in the choir is mean and more like the ordinary method of Common Drawing Room or Tavern painting than that of a church." Whatever be the actual value of the painting on its own merits, as a record faithfully transcribed of very early roof-decoration, it has an interest of its own far beyond much more important work of later periods.

[55]

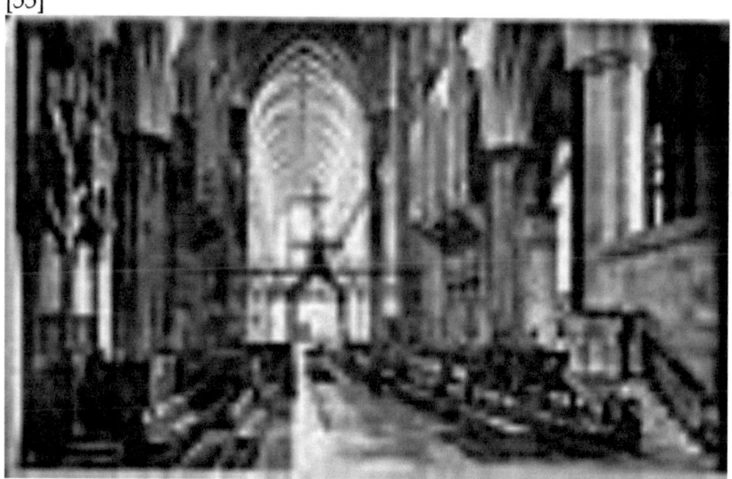

THE CHOIR, LOOKING WEST.
From a Photograph by Messrs. Carl Norman and Co. ToList
[56]

The Choir. — In the second bay from the east, on the north side of the choir, stands the chantry of Bishop Audley, [57] who died in 1524. This excellent example of late Perpendicular work was built by the bishop himself in 1520. Its style is not unlike the chantry of Bishop Fox at Winchester with octagonal shafts, (similar to those of the Salisbury Chapel at Christchurch,) which impart a semi-Oriental touch that is so characteristic of this final development of Gothic art. The images it once enshrined are lost, but the original rich colouring is still distinguishable on the fan tracery of the roof. The arms and initials of its founder are borne on the shields of the cornice. In the corresponding bay on the south side is the chantry founded by Walter Lord Hungerford, in 1429, and removed from the nave in 1778 by his descendant, the Earl of Radnor, who converted it into a family pew. It has been re-decorated, and new emblazonments added. The arms of its founder and his two wives appear on the base. The superstructure is of iron, and a fine example of its class, which includes among the few still extant the chantry of Edward IV. (died 1483) at Windsor, and that of Henry VII. at Westminster Abbey (died 1509). The Audley and Hungerford chantries are the most important left in a cathedral once rich in their kind, as the report of the alienation of their endowments proves.

Of modern fittings, the Brass Lectern was given by members of the late Dean Lear's family. A brass eagle is mentioned by Price, and said to have been given in 1714 at a cost of £160. The pulpit is modern, with carved medallions on its sides.

The bishop's throne, a lofty modern structure, made by Earp of Lambeth, was presented by those clergymen who had been ordained in the cathedral. It replaced one given in 1763.

The Choir Stalls are made up from work of different periods, the seats and elbows being probably part of the original work; the poppy heads of the benches are of the time of Henry VIII. Much later Sir Christopher Wren added to the stalls, and still later Wyatt placed canopies over them, which have since been removed. The dean's seat has been said to be of the time of Charles I.

The Reredos is modern. It was given by Earl Beauchamp in memory of Bishop Beauchamp (1450-81), whose chantry Wyatt swept away. Its design is adapted from the old choir screen, now in the Lady Chapel, and the monument of Bishop Bridport. A large centre panel, eight feet in height, has a bas-relief [58] of the Crucifixion, with the Virgin and St. John; in the head of the central arch are angels amid foliage. On each side are two storied canopied niches, containing statues of the two Maries, and of St. Osmund and Bishop Beauchamp. The whole rises up to a gable terminating in a gemmed and floriated cross. The back facing the Lady Chapel is richly pan- elled. The sides are also elaborately decorated with birds. The de- sign by Sir Gilbert Scott was executed at a cost of about £1,800 by Messrs. Farmer and Brindley.

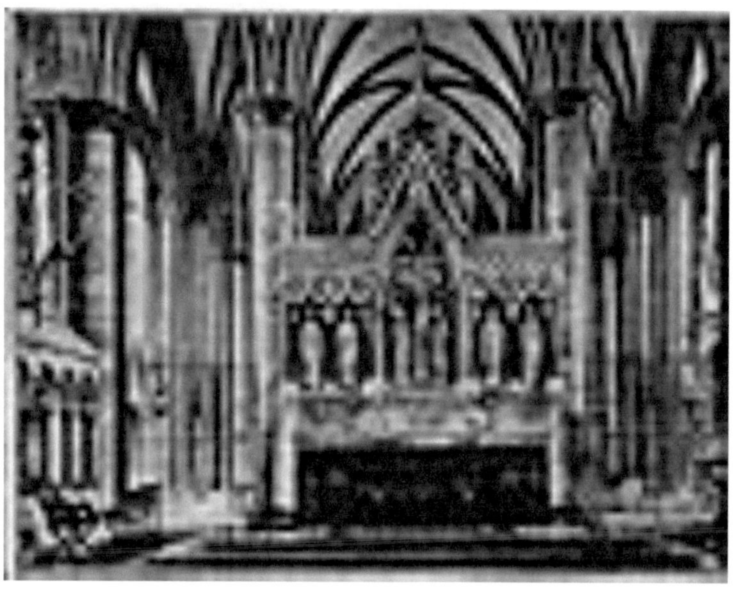

THE HIGH ALTAR AND REREDOS.
From a Photograph by Messrs. Poulton. ToList

The High Altar, the credence table, and sedilia, are excellent ex- amples of modern work. The altar itself is of English oak. Its design comprises an arcade with seven openings, divided into three panels, with much elaborate carving. It was given by those who had re- ceived confirmation at the hands of Bishop Hamilton. The altar cloths, worked and given by Mrs. Sidney Lear, are highly finished examples of modern ecclesiastical needlework. The credence table, of somewhat elaborate design, is of carved oak with a marble top.

The altar rails are of brass, the grills of wrought iron, at each side of the reredos screen the choir partially from the Lady Chapel.

[59]

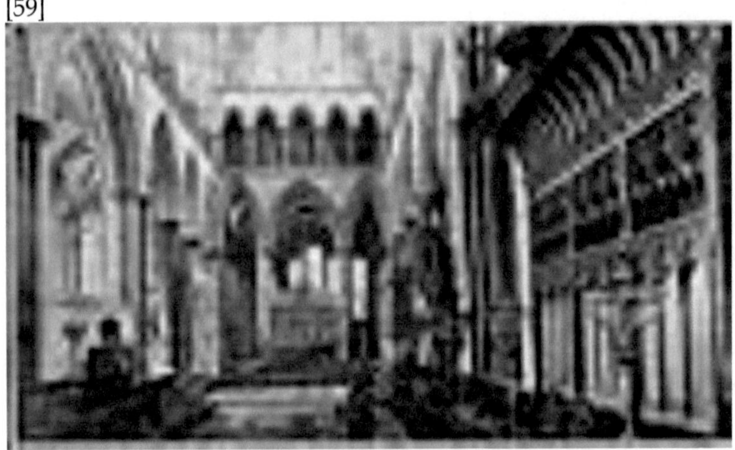

THE CHOIR, LOOKING EAST.
From a Photograph by Messrs. Poulton. ToList
[60]

[61] The definitely planned order of the subjects of the ceiling decoration is held to indicate originally a different place for the high altar than its present site, which is the same as that reported by Leland two hundred years ago, and until attention was drawn to this fact was generally accepted as its original position. From the rood screen the sequence of the figures of the patriarchs and prophets leads up to the climax of "Our Lord in Glory." At this point the capitals of the Purbeck shafts surrounding the pillars supporting the arch on which this figure is painted, are carved in foliage, unlike the others throughout the building, which are invariably moulded only. The whole subject is discussed at length in a paper printed in the "Wilts Archæological Magazine," vol. xvii., in a way that supports the hypothesis advanced. A somewhat important piece of circumstantial evidence came to light during the late restoration, namely a windlass close to the pier on the north side of the supposed original site of the altar, which was possibly intended to raise and lower a baldichino, or ciborium that hung originally over the altar, or still

more probably the pyx, which as many instances show was usually suspended above it.

Possibly the altar was moved when, owing to the early settlement of some of the piers, it was found necessary to wall up the space between the arches opening into the choir transepts, and insert the perpendicular arches as a counter thrust to the strain of the central tower. It is hardly conceivable that the evidence offered by the roof paintings, and the solitary instance of carved capitals, can be misleading on this point.

The East (or **Choir**) **Transept**, which on the north side, screened as it is from the aisle, is used and known also as the Morning Chapel, has on its west wall a portion of a very beautiful screen of Early English work. Of this John Carter, from whose pages the accompanying sketch of a portion is reproduced, says that it was moved during Wyatt's restoration, as he naïvely puts it, "during the late dilapidatious innovations, and modern fanciful introductions so fatal to our study of antiquities." Other authorities consider its original position uncertain. Yet since its architecture is obviously coeval with that of the building, and the arches inserted by Bishop [62] Beauchamp show proof of having been planned to rest on something at the base of the tower piers, there can be little doubt that when Wyatt removed the screen to re-erect a medley of his own composing made of fragments of the demolished chantries, he disturbed one more of the original features of the cathedral.

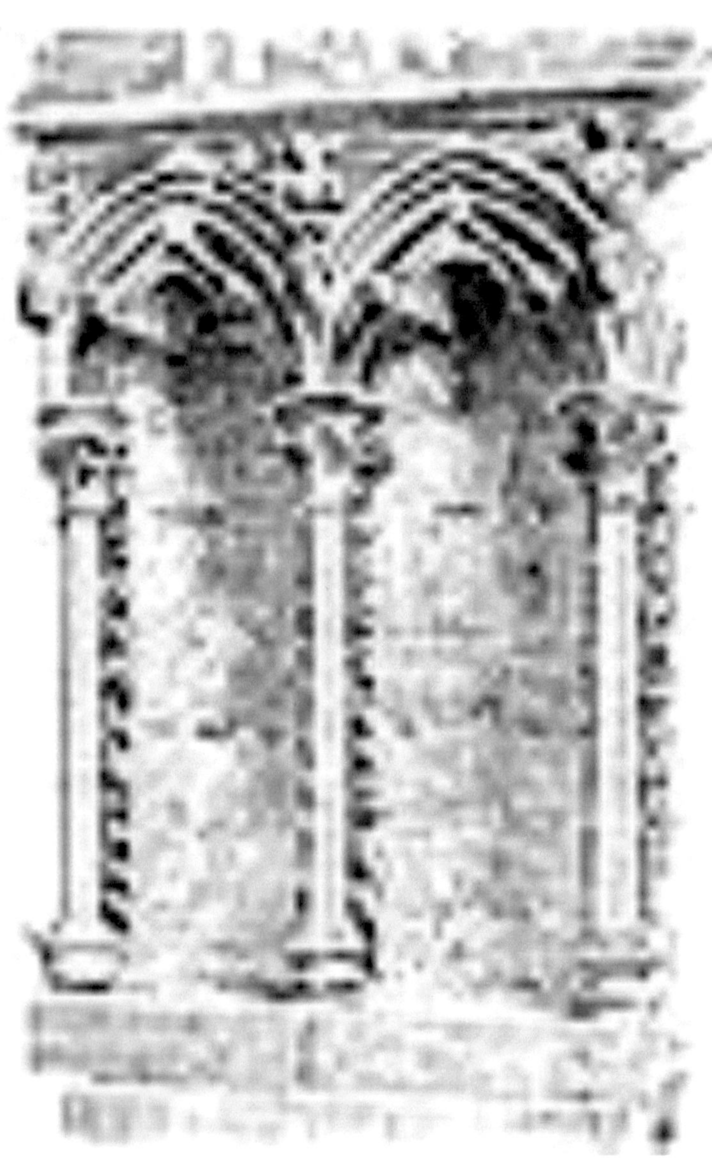

PORTION OF THE OLD ORGAN SCREEN.
From a Drawing by H.P. Clifford. ToList

A curious double aumbry in the north wall of this chapel is unusual, not merely in the pitch of its arches, which are triangular gables, but also in the solid stone shelves dividing its space into six compartments; other aumbries in this church show similar features, but this alone retains its original wooden doors. The superb brass of Bishop Wyville (illustrated on p. 114) [63] is in the pavement of this transept. It is illustrated in almost every work on monumental brasses as a notable example. A canopied lavatory of beautiful design is upon the east wall to the right, the altar being not in the centre, but almost in the corner on the left-hand side.

The Eastern Aisle is not so important as similar "processionals" at Exeter, Winchester, and some other English churches; still, the grace of its clustered columns, like those of the Lady Chapel, give it a character of its own.

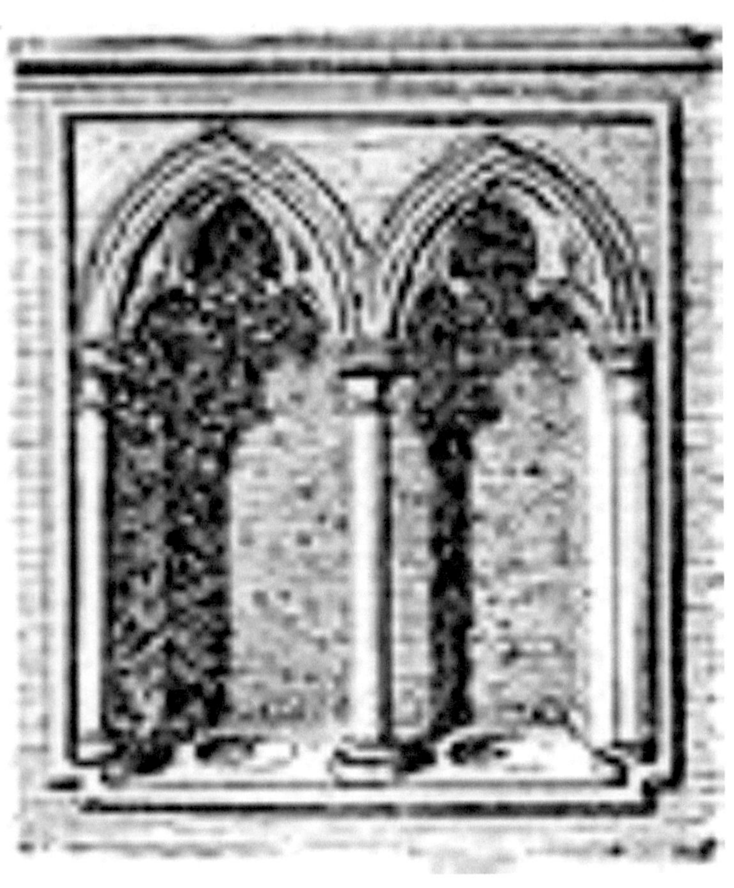

PISCINA IN THE SOUTH CHOIR AISLE. ToList

The Lady Chapel, originally separated from the choir, thrown into the presbytery by Wyatt for the sake of his much overrated vista, is once again partially hidden by the reredos and the grille work of the screen on either side. As the earliest portion of the building, and the only part Bishop Poore lived to see completed, it would not lack interest, were it commonplace in character; but it is on the contrary a particularly graceful example of its time. The whole chapel is divided into a nave and side aisles by single and clustered shafts of Purbeck marble. These extremely slender shafts look unequal to the heavy groined roof they support; for although nearly thirty feet high, the four largest are not quite ten inches in diameter, while the clustered ones are mere rods. Francis Price, whose interest in the building, as he showed throughout his monograph, was that of a practical builder, was "amazed at the vast boldness of the architect, who certainly piqued himself on leaving to posterity an instance of such small pillars bearing so great a load. One would not suppose them," he says, "to stand so firm of themselves as even to resist the force of an ordinary wind." The modern colouring of this part of the building, including the low eastern aisle immediately behind the reredos, is claimed to be an exact restoration of the original, but it is hardly agreeable. The black of the newly polished marble shafts, the dull green of other [64] parts, with the red, green, and white of the vaulting ribs, is more bizarre than beautiful. In regarding traces of mediæval colouring one often forgets that time has blended harmoniously a scheme otherwise entirely crude, and to modern taste unpleasing. How far in English instances this is emphasized by the absence of rich hangings, carpets, vestments, and pictures, it is not within our subject to inquire; but since such restoration of the primitive colouring offends one less in churches that still preserve the more ornate furniture of the Roman Ritual, it is at least a moot point.

The triple lancet east window at the end of the Lady Chapel was filled formerly with stained glass, representing "The Resurrection," after a design by Sir Joshua Reynolds; it is now replaced by modern glass in memory of the late Dean Lear. An altarpiece, composed of fragments of the destroyed Hungerford and Beauchamp Chapels, was set up here by Wyatt. It has lately been replaced by a triptych designed by Sir Arthur Blomfield, with very beautiful panels painted by Mr. Buckeridge. The seven-branched candlesticks in blackwood, silver mounted, are by the same architect. The altar frontal, designed by Mr. Sidney Gambier Parry, and worked by Mrs. Weigall, is so good that it must not be overlooked. The altar itself is of stone from an old altarpiece. Under the windows runs a series of niches, once in the Beauchamp Chapel. Above these rich and delicate canopies, with foliage and fan-tracery springing from corbelled heads, runs an exquisitely sculptured frieze.

In this place, after he was canonized in 1456, the shrine of St. Osmund was erected. His supposed tomb, moved by Wyatt to the nave, is now replaced between the Lady Chapel and the southern aisle. Of the shrine no trace remains; but legends of the miracles worked at it, and the special indulgences granted to the pilgrims who visited it, prove that it existed on this spot. The date MXCIX. inscribed upon this slab has been questioned, on the authority of a diary made by Captain Symons (in 1644), now in the British Museum, in which an entry occurs with reference to this inscription, "a blew stone rising four ynches from the ground, the east end narrower than the west, this lately written Anno MXCIX.," but whether he means to infer that it was lately restored, or that the date itself was a later addition, is not quite clear. The characters of the inscription Planché pointed out correspond in form with those at the time of William the Conqueror, and as sepulchral effigies [65] are uncommon until the middle of the twelfth century, the presumption is in its favour; still it is somewhat pathetic to find that the evidence which serves to connect this otherwise unknown monument with the famous St. Osmund, the greatest figure, not merely of the cathedral, but of the English Church of his time, is not absolutely beyond suspicion. Yet even if the Roman numerals were a later addition, it is hardly credible that the shrine of so popular a saint could have been wrongly identified. When Wyatt, according to his usual habit, explored the interior of the tomb, nothing was found within it.

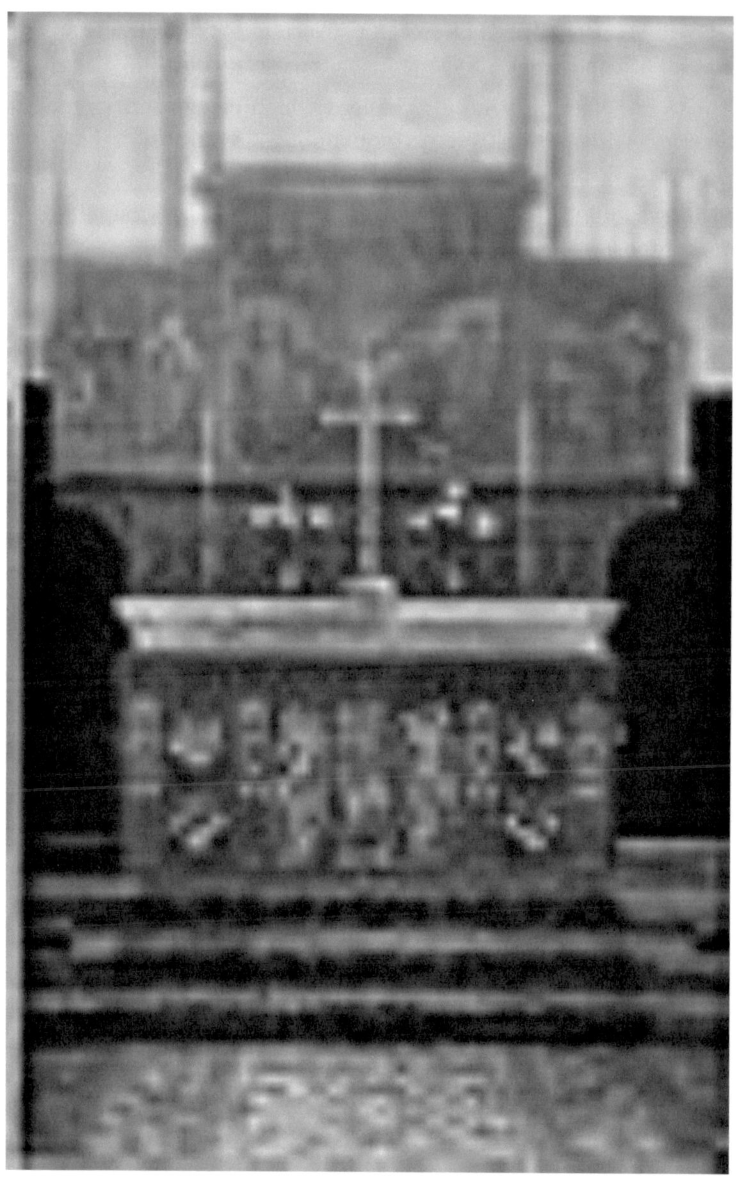

ALTAR AND TRIPTYCH REREDOS IN THE LADY CHAPEL.
From a Photograph by Witcomb and Son, Salisbury. ToList

In 1540 Leland saw here a "ballet," which he transcribes for his Itinerary, with an inscription commanding the faithful to pray for the repose of the soul of Richard Poore.

Monuments in the Transept, Choir and Lady Chapel.—The most important on the west wall of the north great transept is a brass (21) in memory of John Britton, who did so much to revive a taste for archæology and ecclesiastical art by his splendid series of monographs on the cathedrals, and his topographical works. A fine monument of its class is one by Bacon (22), which represents Moral Philosophy mourning over a medallion of James Harris, author of "Hermes" and father of the first Earl of Malmesbury; to whose memory close by is a full-length portrait figure by Chantrey. A figure (23) of Benevolence lifting the veil from a bas-relief of the good Samaritan, by Flaxman, commemorates William Benson Earle, Esq., of the Close, Salisbury. On the north wall of this transept is a canopied effigy (24) of a bishop said to represent John Blythe, who died in 1499. It was originally in the ambulatory of the Lady Chapel, behind the high altar, until Wyatt removed it to its present site. In this transept is the statue (25) to Sir Richard Colt Hoare, author of the "Histories of Modern and Ancient Wiltshire," and other works. It is a seated figure not without dignity, by R.C. Lucas, a native of Salisbury. A portrait bust to Richard Jefferies, with a long and eulogistic inscription, is upon a bracket on the west wall.

Two other monuments by Flaxman deserve notice. That to Walter Long, Esq. (26), a medallion supported by two figures representing Justice and Literature, and one (27) to his brother, William Long, in florid Gothic style, with figures of Science and Benevolence. Dr. Waägen, in his "Art Treasures of Great [66] Britain," says: "The three monuments by Flaxman (in Salisbury) two of which are in Gothic taste, prove that he was superior to most English sculptors in knowledge of the architectonic style. There is nothing extraordinary in the design, but the workmanship is good, and there is real feeling in the heads."

In the north choir aisle, at its junction with the great transept, is a large Purbeck marble altar tomb (28), with panels and tracery, despoiled of the brass legend and armorial bearings it formerly exhibited. This is supposed to have commemorated Bishop Woodville, who died 1484. Two marble slabs that until 1778 were in the floor of this side beneath the first arch of the choir, and in the corresponding place on the south side, have been also stripped of their brasses which showed them to belong to Bishop Simon of Ghent, 1315, and Bishop Mortival, 1330.

On the bench of this aisle is a figure (29) of a skeleton said to represent a man named Fox, who tried to fast forty days. A similar legend is told of the next figure (30), in memory of Dr. Bennett, Precentor of Salisbury (1541 to 1544). It is needless to say that both stories are mere inventions; in many monuments the effigy of the hero commemorated was shown in full pomp above, while in a niche below the skeleton was depicted, by way of pointing a moral too obvious to need further comment.

A brass, in replica of the original, has been reinserted in the marble slab that commemorates Bishop Jewell (1560-71) (31). The next monument (32), for a long time attributed to Bishop Bingham (1229-47), has a flat pointed arch terminating in a decorated finial, above which rises a sort of pyramid of three stories, below is a slab formerly inlaid with brass. Later antiquaries, in spite of the fourteenth century character of its detail, assign it to Bishop Scammel (1284-87). The Audley chapel (33) is entered from this aisle.

In the north-east choir transept aisle are three gravestones of Bishops Wyville (1375), Gheast (1576), and Jewell (1571), removed from the choir when its marble pavement was laid down. In the floor of this transept, which is known also as the morning chapel, is the famous brass to Bishop Wyvill (34), one that has been repeatedly figured in various works on memorial brasses, and it is generally ranked as one of the most interesting [67] of existing examples. Near this is another brass (35) commemorating Bishop Gheast. The lavatory (36) is noticed elsewhere.

In the Lady Chapel, under an arched niche in the north wall, is a coffin-shaped tomb (37) assigned to Bishop Roger, by those who refuse to accept the effigy in the nave as his monument.

The monument (38) at the end of the north aisle of the Lady Chapel is a typical example of the mixed classical style so dear to the early seventeenth century taste. The effigies below its canopy, supported on twisted Corinthian pillars, represent Sir Thomas Gorges and his widow, a maid of honour to Queen Elizabeth. Its medley of obelisks, globes, spheres, and images of the four cardinal virtues is more curious than interesting. Interred near in the choir, and all without monuments are many of the Earls of Pembroke and their wives, including "Sidney's sister, Pembroke's mother."

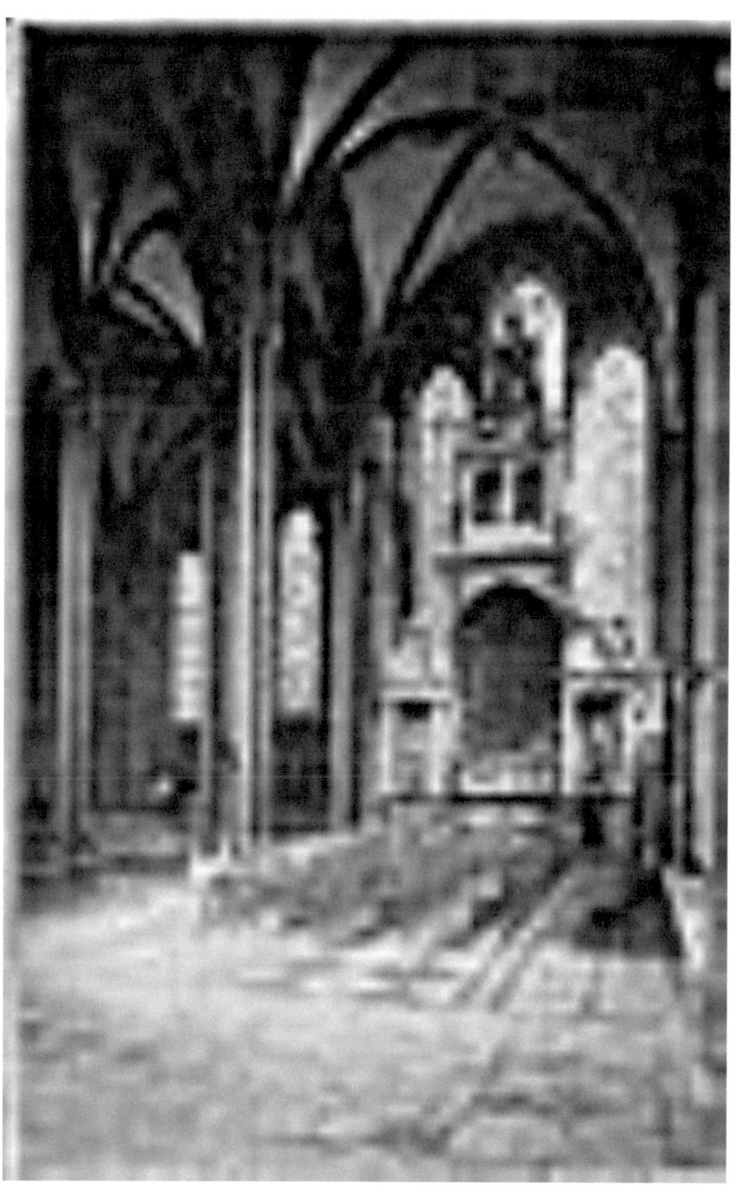

In a niche of the east wall of the choir, behind an arcade of three pointed arches with cinquefoil heads, is a Purbeck marble effigy (39) of a bishop supposed by many to represent Richard Poore. It has been ascribed to Bishop Bingham because its bearded face fails to agree with that depicted on the seal of Bishop Poore, and also because an entry in an old book of records says that he was buried on the north side of the altar. This monument was removed by Wyatt to the north-east transept, to what is supposed to have been its original position. The effigy, whoever it represents, is a fine one, the pastoral crozier of particularly graceful design; above it is an angel supporting the circle of the sun and the crescent of the moon.

The slab which is believed to commemorate St. Osmund (40) is now restored, and placed where his shrine stood formerly, between the south choir aisle and Lady Chapel.

At the east end of the south aisle is the gorgeous monument (41) to Edward, Earl of Hertford, son of the Protector Somerset, uncle of Edward VI., and of his wife Catherine, sister to Lady Jane Grey. The effigies are both in a praying attitude, the Earl in armour. It is elaborately ornamented and splendid in gold and colours, restored by order of the late Duke of Northumberland. It is more ornate than modern taste desires, but still to call it "stately, though tasteless," as does one chronicler, is somewhat harsher criticism than is [68] justified. It is seen in the illustration of the choir aisle given here.

In the south wall is an altar tomb (42), now assigned to William Wilton, Chancellor of Sarum (1506-23). On its cornice are shields bearing the device of Henry VIII. and Catherine of Arragon, a rose and a pomegranate; the arms of Bishop Audley, and those of Abingdon Abbey; also the rebus W.I.L. and a Tun.

The monument (43) to Bishop Moberly, designed by Mr. Arthur Blomfield, is an excellent example of the modern revival. The monument (44) to Bishop Hamilton is also interesting as almost the last design prepared by Sir George Gilbert Scott, and one well worthy of its author.

Next to the Hungerford iron chantry (45) is the monument (46) ordinarily assigned to Bishop William of York, but, like many of the bishops' tombs in this cathedral, without any certain clue to its identity. It consists of a pointed, crocketed arch, terminating in an elaborate finial; with a flat slab below, originally inlaid with a brass.

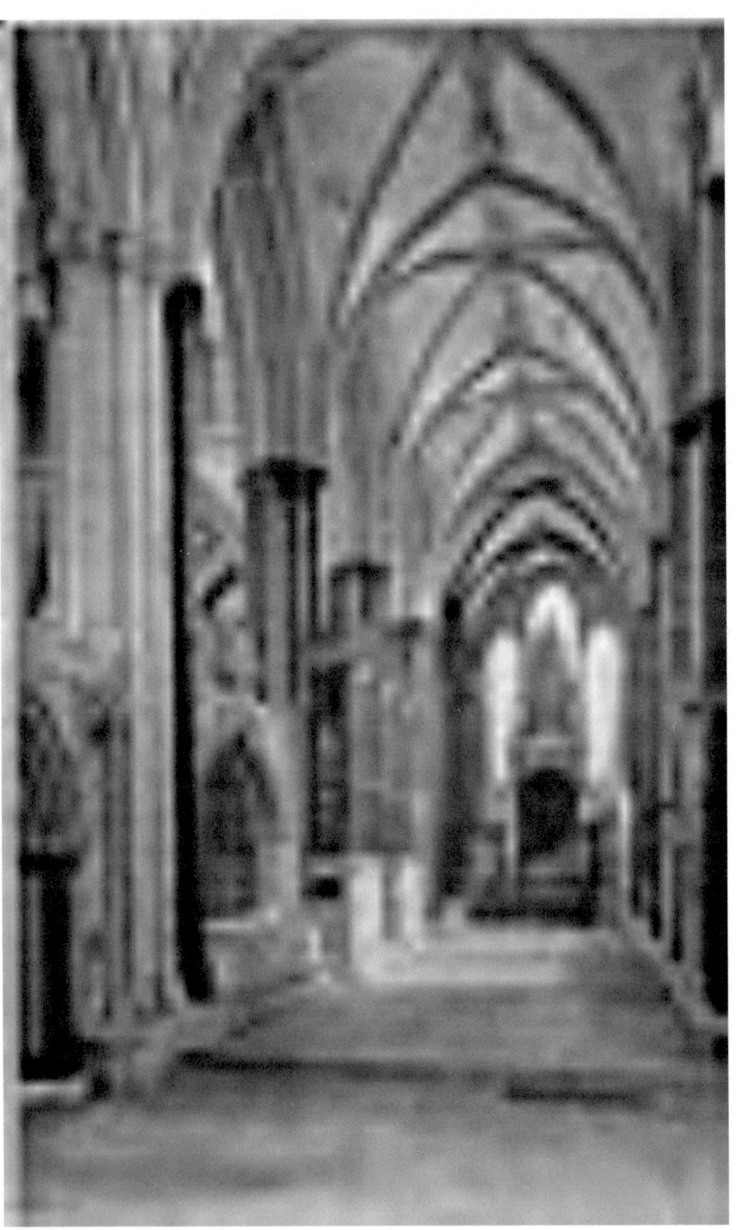

SOUTH CHOIR AISLE, SHOWING THE HUNGERFORD CHAP-
EL.
From a Photograph by S.B. Bolas and Co. ToList

In the south choir transept is the very beautiful chantry (47) to
Bishop Giles de Bridport. On either side the gabled roof is carried
by two open elaborately moulded arches with quatrefoil heads,
inclosing two trefoil arches supported by clustered detached shafts.
Each arch has a triangular hood [69] moulding, crocketed with
carved finials. The spandrils are ornamented with very interesting
carvings. These have been interpreted to mean: on the south side,
the birth of the bishop, his confirmation, his education, and possibly
his first preferment; on the north, the bishop doing homage for his
see, a procession with a cross-bearer (generally accepted as a memorial of the consecration of the building by [70] this bishop); his
death; and finally his soul borne up to heaven by an angel with
outspread wings.

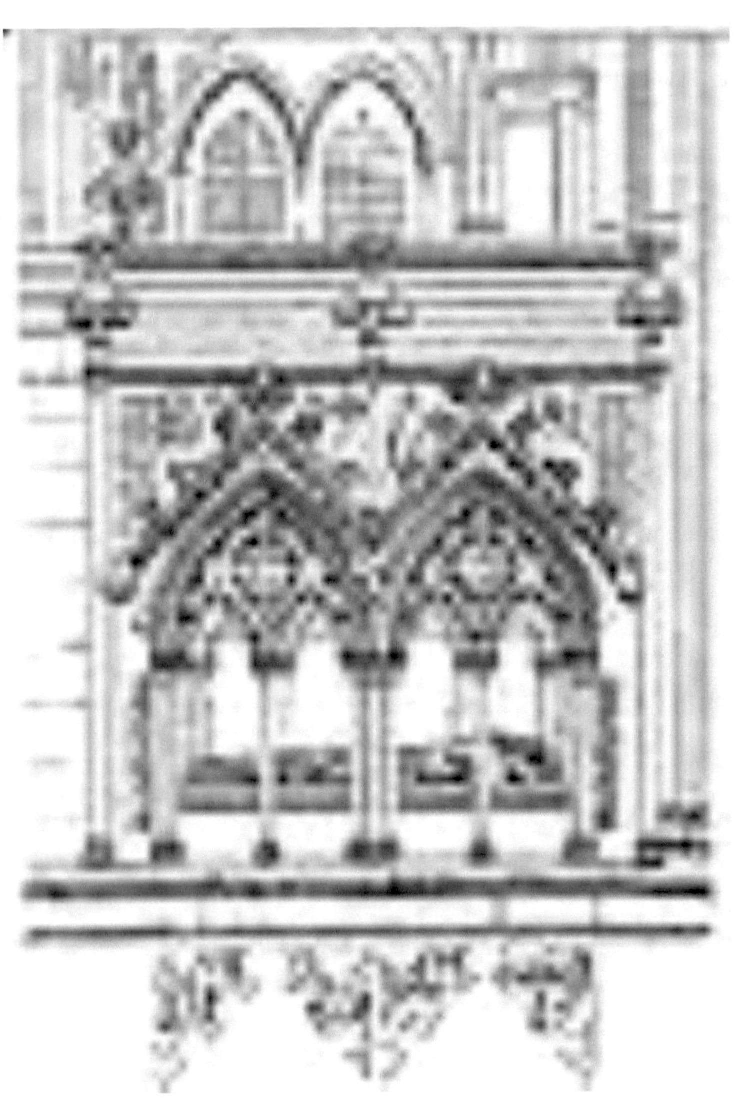

CHANTRY OF BISHOP BRIDPORT.
From Britton's "Cathedrals." ToList

The recumbent effigy has figures of censing angels at its head. The whole style of this exquisite structure is akin to that of the cloisters and the chapter house. The artists who executed the sculptures are believed to have been contemporaries of Niccola Pisano. A chantry was formerly attached to this monument, to the east of which is a double aumbry, or cupboard, for the reservation of the sacrament.

Near this is a tablet to the memory of Canon Bowles, whose edition of Pope plunged him into a bitter controversy with Lord Byron. He was author of many books, including a Life of Bishop Ken. A large modern monument to the late Bishop Burgess is against the south wall. On the west wall is the monument (48) of Bishop Seth Ward, whose additions to the palace, after the Restoration, are mentioned elsewhere. The Izaak Walton, whose gravestone is near, was the son of the famous angler. Near is one to the memory of the father of the poet Young, and a modern tablet to Richard Hooker, author of "Ecclesiastical Polity."

In the south choir aisle is a rather interesting monument (51) to Bishop Davenant, who is usually credited with the honour of being one of the translators of the Bible. It is of white marble with two black Corinthian pillars, surmounted by a mitre and arms. There is also a tablet in coloured relief to the memory of Mrs. Wordsworth, wife of the bishop; and a brass, cruciform in shape, inserted in a polished granite slab, which forms a memorial to Canon Liddon.

Many other monuments of ancient and modern date that concern forgotten celebrities, or are of purely local interest, cannot be catalogued. Nor is it needful to insist on morals they mostly enforce, that really all recent works of this class lack the dignity which has given the word monumental a new meaning.

On the bench opposite is the monument (52), an altar tomb with shields and initials, of Bishop Salcot (or Capon), whose notoriety as a "time-serving courtier" is mentioned in another chapter.

A pseudo-classical monument near (53), with vine-leaves and grapes in green and gold entwined round black Corinthian pillars, is to the memory of Sir Richard Mompesson, knight, [71] who is represented in armour, and Dame Katherine, his wife, clad in black robe with gold flowers.

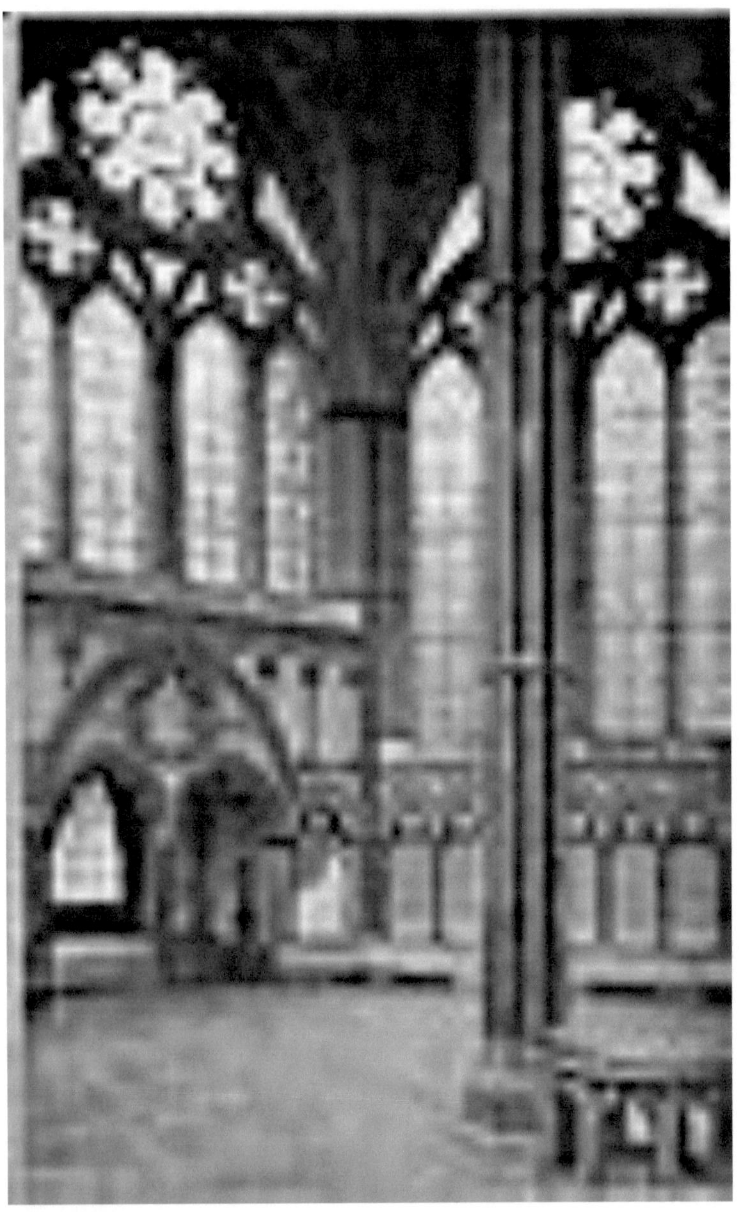

THE CHAPTER HOUSE.
From a Photograph by Carl Norman and Co. ToList

Close to the south transept, in the choir aisle, is the altar tomb (54) of Bishop Mitford, 1407, which Britton rightly calls a noble monument. In the spandrils of the flat arch of its canopy are armorial shields. Lilies and birds, holding in their beaks scrolls, inscribed, "Honor Deo et gloria," are on its cornice. The shields on the north bear the bishop's arms and those of his see; on the south are quartered the arms of England and France, and the ensign of Edward the Confessor — the cross *patonée* surrounded by five martlets.

Here also is a modern altar tomb (55), from a design by Mr. G.E. Street, to the memory of John Henry Jacob, and a fine Jacobean monument with bust and Latin inscription to Lord Chief Justice Hyde.

Among many other post-reformation monuments are those to: Bishop Fisher (56) on the east wall; a canopied altar tomb (57) in the Gothic style to the memory of Edward and Rachel Poore (died 1780 and 1781), the collateral descendants of the famous bishop, and a marble slab set in a Gothic frame to Canon Hume (died 1834).

On the south wall of the nave (58) there is an effigy of Mrs. Eleanor Sadler, who died July 30th, 1622, and was interred "according to her owne desire under this her pew, wherein with great devotion she had served God dailie almost L years." Amid other monuments on this wall, dating from late in the seventeenth century to the present day, is a small tablet (60) to one of the most famous Salisbury men in modern times, the Right Hon. Henry Fawcett, M.P., late Postmaster-General, who died in 1884.

The Chapter House, which is entered from the eastern walk of the cloisters, dates probably from the time of Edward the First; later it may be, but certainly not earlier than the commencement of his reign, as, during certain excavations for underpinning the walls in 1854, several pennies of that king were found below its foundations. The architecture is somewhat later in style than that of the cloisters, and if it be not, as its admirers claim, the most beautiful in England, it has few rivals. Like Westminster, Wells, and other English examples, except York and Southwell, it has a central pillar, from which the groining of the roof springs gracefully in harmonious [72] lines.

A raised bench of stone runs round the interior. At its back, forty-nine niches of a canopied arcade borne on slight Purbeck marble shafts mark out as many seats. They are apportioned as follows: those at each side of the entrance to the Chancellor and Treasurer respectively, the rest to the Bishop, Dean, Arch-deacons, and other members of the chapter.

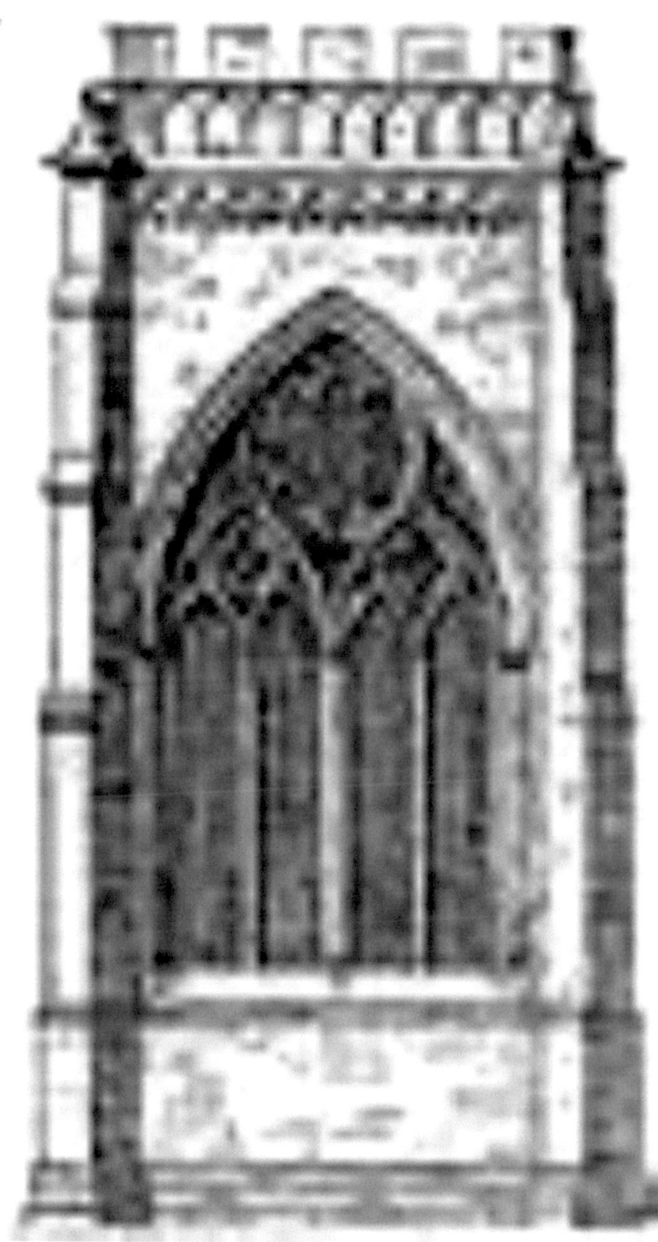

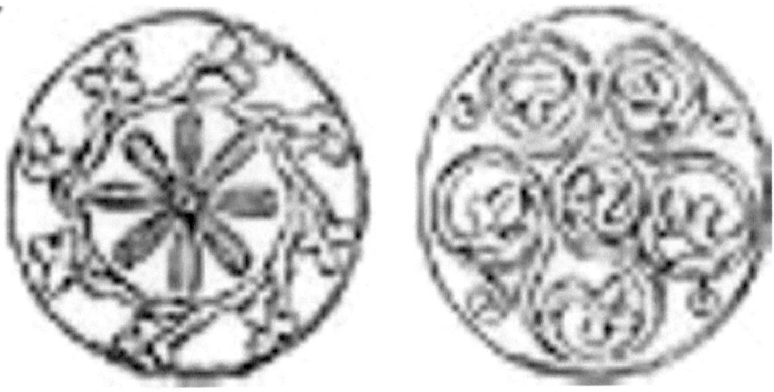

BOSSES FROM THE CHAPTER HOUSE ROOF.

The plan of the building is octagonal, about fifty-eight feet in diameter and fifty-two feet in height. Each side has a large fanlight window with traceried head. Below these windows and above the canopies of the seats is a very remarkable series of bas-reliefs, noticed more fully later on. The bosses of the roof are somewhat elaborately carved; one north of the west doorway has groups of figures on it, apparently intended to represent armourers, musicians, and apothecaries, possibly commemorating guilds who were benefactors to the building; the others have foliage chiefly with grotesque monsters. On the base of the central pillar is a series of carvings taken probably from one of the many books of fables so popular in the middle ages. These [73] [74] [75] were reproduced from the originals, which are preserved in the cloisters.

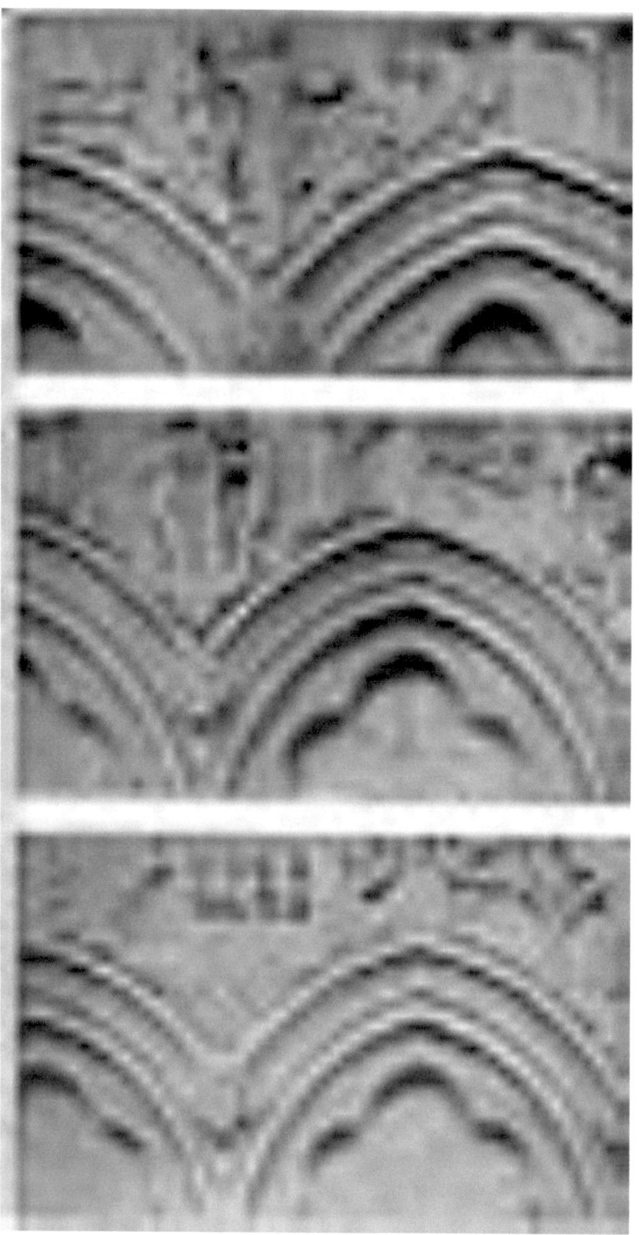

DETAILS OF SCULPTURES IN THE CHAPTER HOUSE.
From Photographs by Catherine Weed Ward. ToList

   The quatrefoil over the doorway has an empty niche, and it is not possible to say with certainty whether it was originally filled by a crucifix, as Mr. Mackenzie Walcott infers from the symbols of the Evangelists in the angles of the panel; or, with a seated figure of our Lord in majesty; or, as a third archæologist has suggested, a coronation of the Virgin. Filling the voussoirs of the arch of the doorway are fourteen small niches containing subjects from the Psychomachia of Prudentius, the Battle of the Virtues against the Vices. The figures are not easily identified, but Mr. Burges, whose "Iconography of the Chapter House" is the most important monograph on the subject, suggests that on the right-hand side the figures in the third niche from the top appear to represent Concord triumphing over Discord; in the sixth, Temperance is pouring liquor down the throat of Intemperance; on the seventh, Fortitude tramples on Terror, who cuts her own throat. On the left hand in the first niche Faith is trampling on Infidelity; in the second, a Virtue covers a Vice with her cloak, while the Vice embraces her knees with one hand and stabs her with a sword held in the other. This incident is taken from Prudentius: "Discord by stealth wounds Concord; she is taken and killed by" Faith, which latter incident may be represented in the next compartment. In the fourth niche, Truth pulls out Falsehood's tongue; in the fifth, Modesty scourges Lust; in the sixth, Generosity pours coin into the throat of Avarice. To quote the words of the author from whom these interpretations are derived: "These sculptures are of the very highest class of art, and infinitely superior to any work in the chapter house; the only defect is the size of the heads: probably this was intentional on the part of the artist. The intense life and movement of the figures are worthy of special study." These allegories are common in paintings and sculptures of this period; at Canterbury the same subjects are incised on the pavement that surrounds the shrine of St. Thomas à Becket.

   On the spandrils of the continuous arcade, sculptures in high relief once restored as far as possible in the original colours are now again scraped clean, and with the new heads to the figures look so modern that it is hard to believe they are contemporary with the building they adorn, yet since on the whole the [76] restoration has been faithfully accomplished they may be studied as peculiarly valuable examples of early mediæval sculpture, showing certain naïve qualities that raise them far above the usual level of contemporary work. They are supposed to have been defaced by the Commission sitting in this building during the time of the Rebellion. The subjects are:

West Wall.

 1. A Representation of Chaos.
 2. The Creation of the Firmament.

North-west Wall.

 3. The Creation of the Earth.
 4. The Creation of the Planets.
 5. The Creation of the Birds and Fishes.
 6. The Creation of Adam and Eve.
 7. The Seventh Day.
 8. The First Marriage.
 9. The Temptation of Eve.
10. Adam and Eve hiding.

North Wall.

11. The Flight from Paradise.
12. The First Labour.
13. Cain and Abel's Offering.
14. The First Murder.
15. The Punishment of Cain.
16. The Command to Noah.
17. The Ark.
18. The Vineyard of Noah.

North-east Wall.

19. Noah's Drunkenness.
20. The Building of Babel.
21. Angels appearing to Abraham.
22. Abraham entertaining the Angels.

23. The Destruction of the Cities of the Plain.
24. Lot's Escape.
25. Abraham and Isaac.
26. The Sacrifice of Isaac.

East Wall.

27. Isaac and Jacob.
28. Esau and Isaac.
29. Rebecca and Jacob.
30. Jacob and Rachel.
31. Rachel, Jacob, and Laban.
32. Jacob and the Angels.
33. The Angel touching Jacob's thigh.
34. Jacob meeting Esau.

South-east Wall.

35. Joseph's Dream.
36. Joseph relating his Dream.
37. Joseph in the Pit.
38. Joseph sold into Egypt.
39. Joseph's Coat brought to Jacob.
40. Joseph and Potiphar.
41. Potiphar's Wife.
42. Joseph accused.

South Wall.

43. Joseph in Prison.
44. Pharaoh's Baker and Butler.
45. Pharaoh's Dream.
46. Pharaoh's Indecision.
47. Joseph before Pharaoh.
48. Joseph as Ruler.
49. Joseph's Brethren.
50. The Cup placed in Benjamin's Sack.

South-west Wall.

51. The Discovery of the Cup.
52. His Brethren before Joseph.
53. Jacob on his Way to Egypt.
54. Joseph and his Brethren pleading.

55. Joseph protecting his Brethren.
56. Moses on Sinai.
57. The Miracle of the Red Sea.
58. The Destruction of the Egyptians.

   West Wall.

59. Moses striking the Rock.
60. The Law declared.

[77]

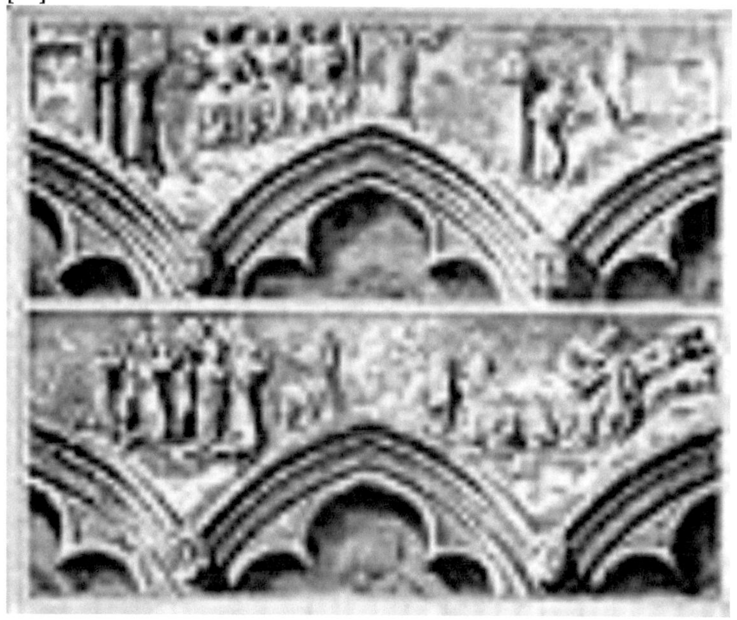

SCULPTURE IN THE CHAPTER HOUSE. ToList

[78]

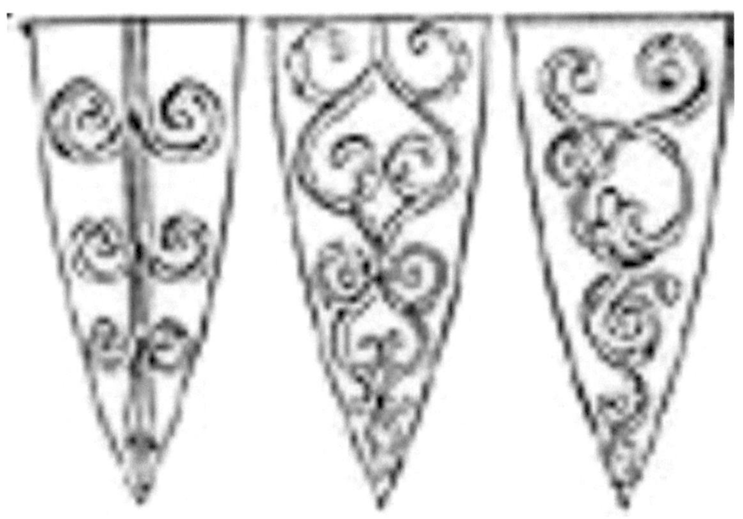

DECORATIONS IN THE GROINING OF THE CHAPTER
HOUSE. ToList

[79] The modern decoration of the chapter house includes stained
glass of a geometrical pattern in the eight windows, which, if not
peculiarly good, is harmless enough. Some diaper wall painting,
shown in the photograph reproduced here, which until lately decorated the back of the arcade is now entirely cleaned off. The tiles of
the floor have been reproduced from the designs of the original
Norman pavement. The vaulted roof is re-painted in exact accordance with its original design. The marble shafts of the arcade are repolished, and the central shaft has also been re-worked to a smooth
surface. Gilding has been applied freely to the bosses of the roof and
the capitals of the pillars. The ancient table, shown in the engraving,
has also been restored; it is a very interesting specimen of early
decorated furniture.

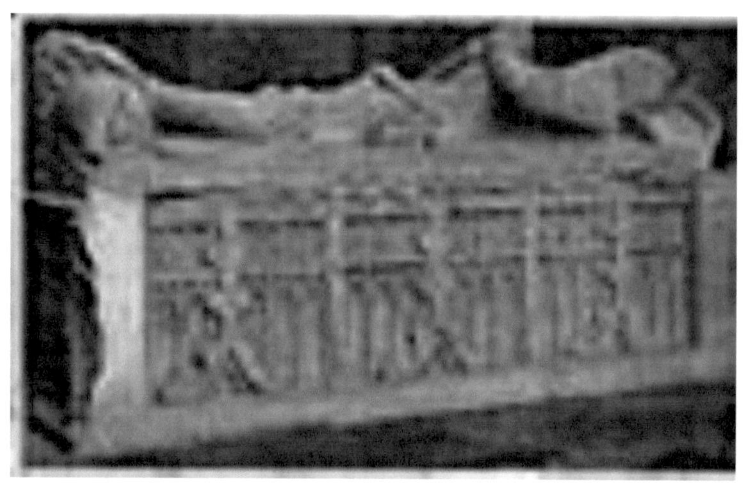

TOMB OF SIR JOHN MONTACUTE.
From a Photograph by Catherine Weed Ward. ToList

FOOTNOTES:

[7] "The Century Magazine," March, 1888.

[8] The numerals in brackets refer to the position of each monument as shown on the plan.

[9] In 1448 Nicholas Upton the precentor tried to limit the choice of the choristers to three candidates selected by the chapter; but this attempt to curtail their privilege was successfully resisted by the boys.

[80]

THE CATHEDRAL PRECINCTS.

The common practice of writers who are describing any one of our more important cathedrals is to declare that altogether it may be fairly called the most beautiful. So great is the fascination exercised by continual study of a single mediæval building which has escaped destruction, or over-restoration, that such a statement may be advanced in all good faith. In claiming, however, that the cloisters of Salisbury are on the whole the most beautiful in England, it is merely re-asserting what many critics of Gothic architecture have already decided to be true. The cloisters of Gloucester are far richer, the space they cover at Wells (like Salisbury, not a monastic establishment) is greater, and in other details these may not be the finest. But, as a whole, their beautiful proportion and the general symmetry of their design make them worthy adjuncts to a building which is pre-eminent for these special qualities.

Situated, according to the usual custom, on the south-west side of the cathedral, with their western wall in a line with its west front, they are exceedingly picturesque. Even so far back as the time of Leland, we find him declaring that "the cloister on the south side of the church is one of the largest and most magnificent in Britain." Yet, as a recent critic has observed, from a purely technical point of view, there is "too great a mass of blank wall above the arcade." The green sward of the large garth, 140 feet square, with its covered walks, 181 feet long, on each side, and the fine group of cedars in the centre, showing against the cool grey of the stonework realize the ideal of that cloistered solitude so dear to the poets; it should not be forgotten, however, that the arrangements of this cathedral are not monastic, for it was never aught but a collegiate building. The style is late thirteenth century with windows of exceedingly graceful design; double arches with quatrefoils above, united in pairs with a large six-foiled circle in the main head. The [81] upper portions of the tracery had, not so long ago, traces of coloured glass here and there, but whether this feature was part of the original scheme is very doubtful. The shafts, originally of Purbeck marble (replaced in 1854 by stone) both between and in the centres of the windows have simply moulded capitals; while those of the clustered columns at the main angles are carved. Modern opinion is inclined to date the beginning of the work between 1260 to 1284; but so late as 1338, as a dated charter in Bishop Wyville's time which refers to the enlargement of the cloisters shows, they were not quite completed; hence it is inferred that a part, possibly only one side, was built at first. The north arcade is entirely independent of the south wall of the nave, the long space between being known as the Plumbery. The garth is used as a burial ground, and in the cloisters are many monuments, but none of more than local interest, except possibly a tablet to the memory of Francis Price (died Mar. 20th, 1753, aged 50), the cathedral architect, whose excellent monograph devoted to the building is still one of the most useful books of reference on the subject. The [82] drawing here reproduced from Britton's "Salisbury," shows the work before its restoration by Bishop Denison; but it has been chosen because it suggests the peculiar beauty of the place better than any photograph. From the cloisters a very charming glimpse of the spire may be obtained.

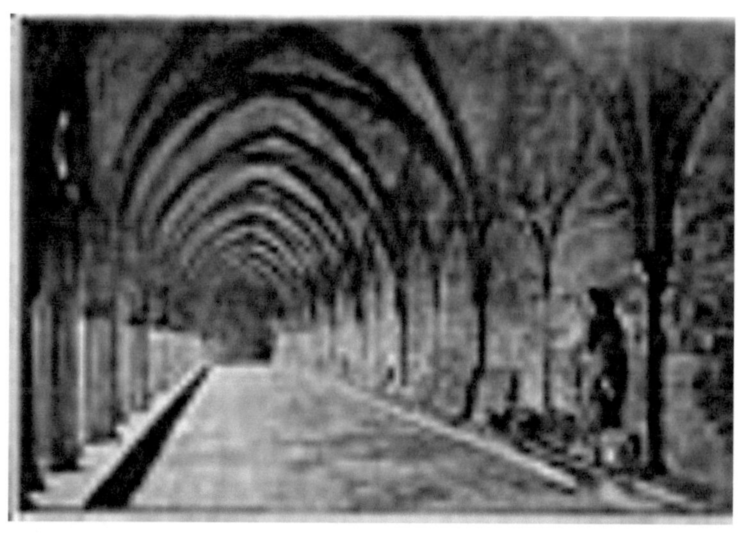

THE CLOISTERS.
From a Photograph by Messrs. Poulton. ToList

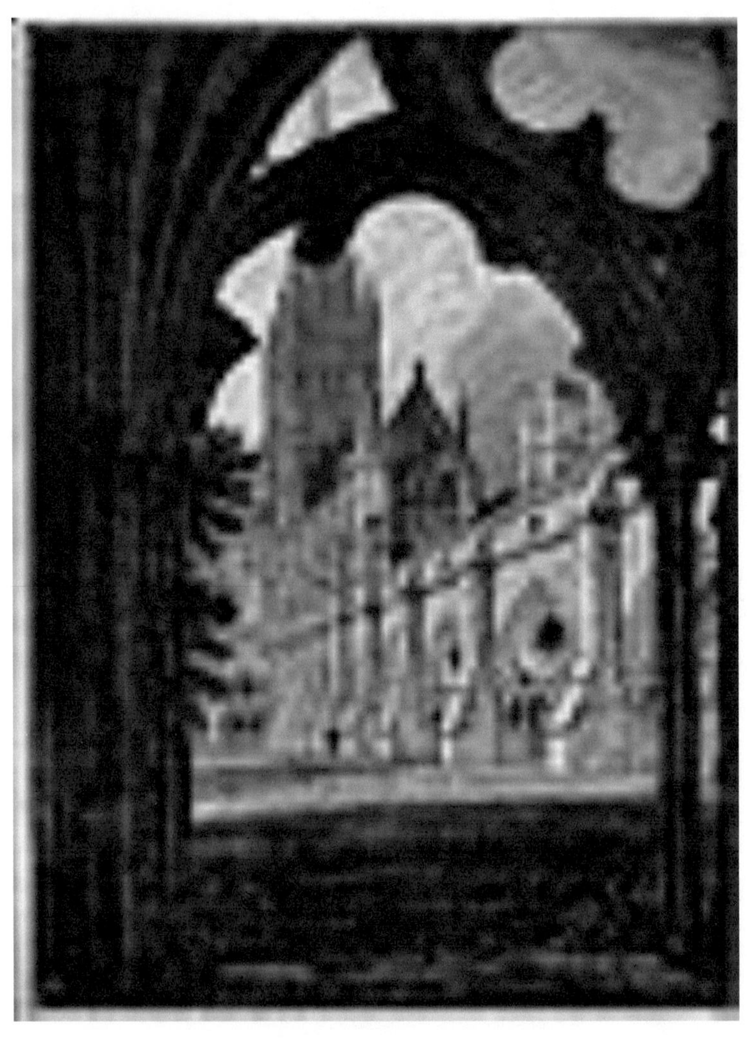

THE CLOISTERS, LOOKING NORTH. ToList

The **Library** occupying the upper story that extends over part of the eastern arcade is an important collection, its manuscripts alone filling a hundred and eighty-seven volumes. These (with one exception, bequeathed by Bishop Denison, a splendidly illuminated breviary *circa* A.D. 1460, containing among other specially interesting matter the order of service for the installation of the Boy-bishops,) have been in the possession of the [83] dean and chapter at least four hundred years, and range in date, according to the best authorities, from the ninth to the fourteenth centuries.

Among the most important is (No. 150) A Psalter, of the Gallican Version, on vellum, 160 folios, tenth century. The decorations of this MS. are somewhat rude, the initials and colouring throughout being chiefly in red. Internal evidence fixes its date about A.D. 969. A Psalter (No. 180) on 173 folios, contains in parallel columns the Gallican and Hebrew of Jerome's translation, and other matter, with ornamental initials and devices; a Lectionary on vellum, 190 folios (No. 153) is a finely written manuscript, with elaborate initials in gold and colours, this is about A.D. 1277. A fifteenth century "Processional for the Use of Sarum," on vellum, 50 folios (No. 148) contains some entries that throw light on various local customs, as for example, the distribution of the carpet used in the enthronement of the bishop, which was laid from *ostio hospicii agni* to the altar in the treasury. The unique "Tonale secundum usum Sarum" bound with an "Ordinale secundum usum Sarum" (No. 175) is of the fourteenth century, on 214 folios of vellum. In a volume (No. 39) is a copy of the Gospel of Nicodemus in an English version beginning, "Whanne Pylatus was reuler and justyse of ye Jewerye, and Rufus and Leo were consuls." Another book of more than ordinary interest is Chaucer's translation of Boethius' "De Consolatione Philosophiæ," on vellum in double columns, fifteenth century. A twelfth century MS. of the "Historia Regum Brittaniæ," by Geoffrey de Monmouth (No. 121); and the "Historia Miscella" of Paul Warnefrid, are among many others that deserve mention.

Among the printed books of the Library are about a score belonging to the fifteenth century, and one hundred of the sixteenth. Some of these are of extreme rarity. In a copy of Sibbes' "Returning Backslider" is this couplet (attributed to Doddridge) in the handwriting, with autograph, of Isaac Walton:

> "Of this blest man let this just praise be given,
> Heaven was in him before he was in heaven."

Bishop Gheaste was a benefactor to the library, and left it a large legacy, the foundation of the present collection of printed books.

[84] The library is shown to the public on certain days, and the clergy of the diocese have the privilege of borrowing books therefrom.

According to the "Inventory of the Riches of the Cathedral Church of Sarum," made by Master Thomas Robertson, treasurer of the same church in 1536, 28th year of Henry VII., we find images, "of God the Father with our Saviour young, of silver and gilt with gold, ornate with red stones weighing 74 ounces." Others of Our Lady, including a "grate and fair ymage sitting in a chaire ... her child sits in her lap very costly and fair to look upon." Reliques of the 11,000 virgins, in four purses; Pyxides of Ivory of Chrystal, and silver gilt, "Cruces" of Gold and Silver. And a great Cross silver and gilt with images on the crucifix, Mary and John, and the left part of the cross — weighing 180 ounces. Calices (chalices), Fereta, Candelabra, Philateria, Tabernucla, Ampulæ, Thuribula, Chrismatones, Copes and Chasubles, Mitres, Basons, Garlands, and hangings, Morses and many other items. Also the textus, which was given by Hubert de Burgh, here described as "A text after Matthew having images of St. Joseph, and our Lady and our Saviour all in a bed of straw, in every corner is the image of an apostle," and a huge list of items not merely interesting in themselves, but as evidence of the wealth of the cathedral.

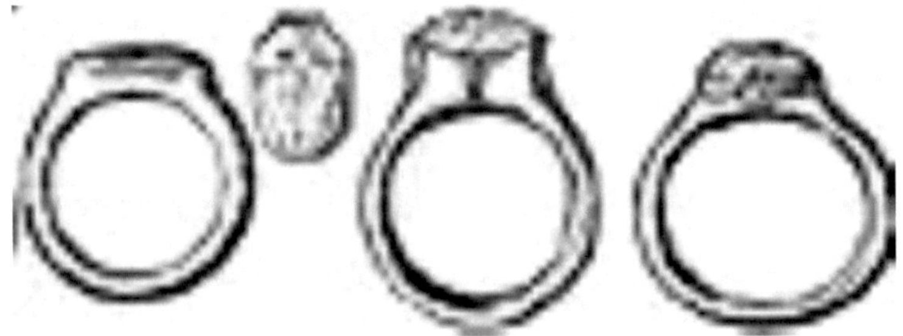

RINGS FOUND IN THE LADY CHAPEL. ToList

The Muniment Room, which is approached from the south choir transept, is part of a two-storied building, octagonal in plan. The ground floor, formerly the sacristy, is now used as a vestry for the canons; the upper one, a dimly-lighted room, with an oak roof supported by a central column of wood, is the muniment chamber. Traces of a cross on the central pillar support the theory that the "Altar in the Treasury," referred to in various early documents, stood here. The solidity and strength of the building, and the fact that it was undoubtedly the store house for the vestments and treasures of the church, leaves little doubt that the supposition is true.

[85] A very fine cope chest, reproduced by Mr. William Burges in his "Architectural Drawings," 1870, until lately preserved in the vestry, now in the north choir aisle, has a quaintly-carved capital on one of its shafts that suggests a very early date for its construction. The heavy lid was originally lifted by a rope and windlass. Although possessing no traces of painting or gilding, and but little carving, it is both curious and interesting as a specimen of woodwork coeval with the cathedral itself. A somewhat similar one exists in Westminster Abbey, in both the lifting lids worked on very slight pivots. At Westminster the chains remain. In 1834 a writer described the room as "a feast for moths and spiders;" now it is kept in admirable order. The most important of its extremely valuable documents have been printed in a volume devoted to Sarum in the "Master of the Rolls Series," in the late Canon Jones' "Fasti Ecclesiæ: Sarisberiensis." In addition to these historic papers there is an immense quantity of Chapter Registers and other MSS. of more local interest. Many of the chests and presses date from early times, when the three keys needed to open each were severally in the charge of three of the cathedral dignitaries. The contemporary copy of Magna Charta, made for William Longespée, first Earl of Salisbury, and referred to elsewhere, is sometimes exhibited here.

The documents which contain "the statutes and ordinances" by which the cathedral is governed, extend over six centuries, commencing in 1091 and ending 1697. These were edited by Dr. Edward A. Dayman, and the late Rev. W.H. Rich Jones, Vicar of Bradford-on-Avon, whose researches in the past history of not merely the cathedral, but the whole district, were so extended, that it is impossible to do justice in every instance to many facts which have been taken from his pages in the preparation of this handbook. The privately printed volume, published in 1883, contains the Latin text with English notes of these various documents. The details of most of these, although of immense value to antiquarians, are too technical to be available for quotation here, but the indirect allusions to customs and manners of the past, makes many a paragraph pleasant reading, although the whole document may refer to merely the working details of administration. The statute, dated A.D. 1319, relating to the rights of the boy bishop, is one of the few that have more than local interest.

[86]

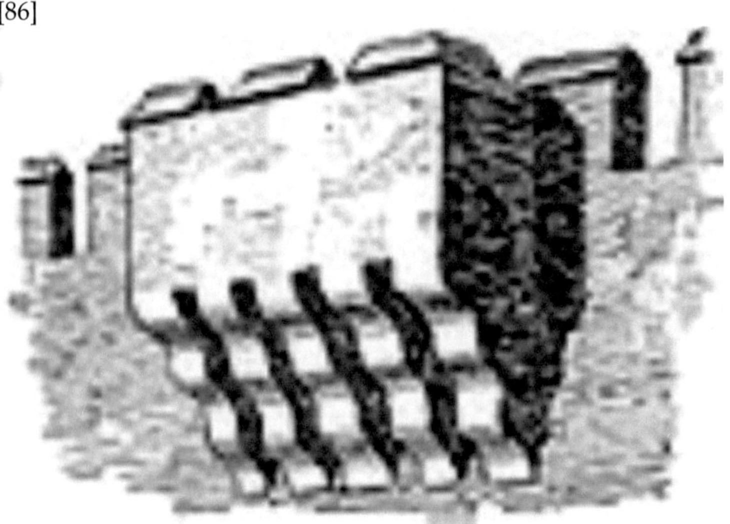

HANGING PARAPET ON THE EAST WALL OF THE CLOSE.
ToList

The Close is certainly a fit setting for the jewel it surrounds, and with full remembrance of the superb position of Durham, the picturesque eminence of Lincoln, the dignity that marks the isolated hill whereon Ely towers over the fens around it, the harmonious environment of Wells, and many another site made memorable by its cathedral, Salisbury is, in its own way, not less beautiful. The quiet tranquillity of the large lawn, the half-hidden houses that nestle among its trees, the sense of being completely shut off from the work-a-day world, impress one as much as the apparent vastness of the area thus devoted to the cathedral. Leland, in his "Itinerary," was equally struck with its beauty, although, as the frontispiece shows, the surroundings were very different before Wyatt's exploits, and probably in Leland's time preserved still more of their mediæval aspect. He says: "The great and large embatelid waulle of the palace having 3 gates to entre into it thus namyd: the close gate as principale by north ynto the town, Saint Anne's gate by est, and Harnham gate by south toward Harham bridge. The close wall was never ful finished as in one place evidently apperith I redde that in Bishop Rogers days as I remembere a convention was between him and the Canons of Saresbyri de Muro clausi."

Whether the builders of our great churches were conscious of the beauty of their surroundings, or whether no little of that loveliness is but the slow result of centuries of care and the accident of natural growth, need not be discussed. That to an American especially this peculiar beauty tells with great force we can readily believe, and Mrs. Van Rensselaer, whose paper on Salisbury has been quoted before in this book, expresses admirably the feeling, which, whether it be true or only imaginary, is no doubt the impression of such a place as the Close of Salisbury on many an educated visitor. "Salisbury," [87] she writes, "is the very type and picture of the Church of the Prince of Peace. Nowhere else does a work of Christian architecture so express purity and repose and the beauty of holiness, while the green pastures that surround it might well be those of which the Psalmist writes. When the sun shines on the pale grey stones, and the level grass, and the silent trees, and throws the long shadow of the spire across them, it is as though a choir of seraphs sang in benediction of that peace of God which passeth understanding. The men who built and planted here were sick of the temples of Baalim, tired of being cribbed and cabined, weary of quarrelsome winds and voices. They wanted space and sun, and stillness, comfort and rest, and beauty, and the quiet ownership of their own; and no men ever more perfectly expressed, for future times to read, the ideal they had in mind."

The **Bell Tower**, a striking feature of the close as it was before 1789, is shown on page 19, in the facsimile of an engraving originally published in 1761, and re-engraved in the superb County History in 1804(?). This shows the campanile standing at the north-west corner of the inclosure.

In style it was about the same period as the chapter house and cloisters. The plan appears to have been square, although one writer, frequently quoted, calls it multangular; the stone tower was in two massive stories with lancet windows in the lower, and windows with plate tracery above, with a spire apparently of wood crowning the whole. Leland speaks of it as "a notable and strong square tower for great belles, and a pyramis on it, in the cemiterie." It was evidently massive enough to have stood for centuries, and the single pillar of Purbeck marble, "lying in its natural bed," which was the central support that carried the bells, the belfry, and the spire, is specially mentioned by Price as perfectly sound, but he owns that the leaden spire, and a wooden upper story, were decayed, and puts forward a design of a sham classic dome which he hopes might be erected in its place. When the cathedral was visited in 1553 by the Royal Commission there remained a peal of ten bells, and the re-casting in 1680 of the seventh and eighth by the Purdues, local founders, is recorded among the muniments. The sixth is now the clock bell of the cathedral, but the fate of the others is absolutely unknown.

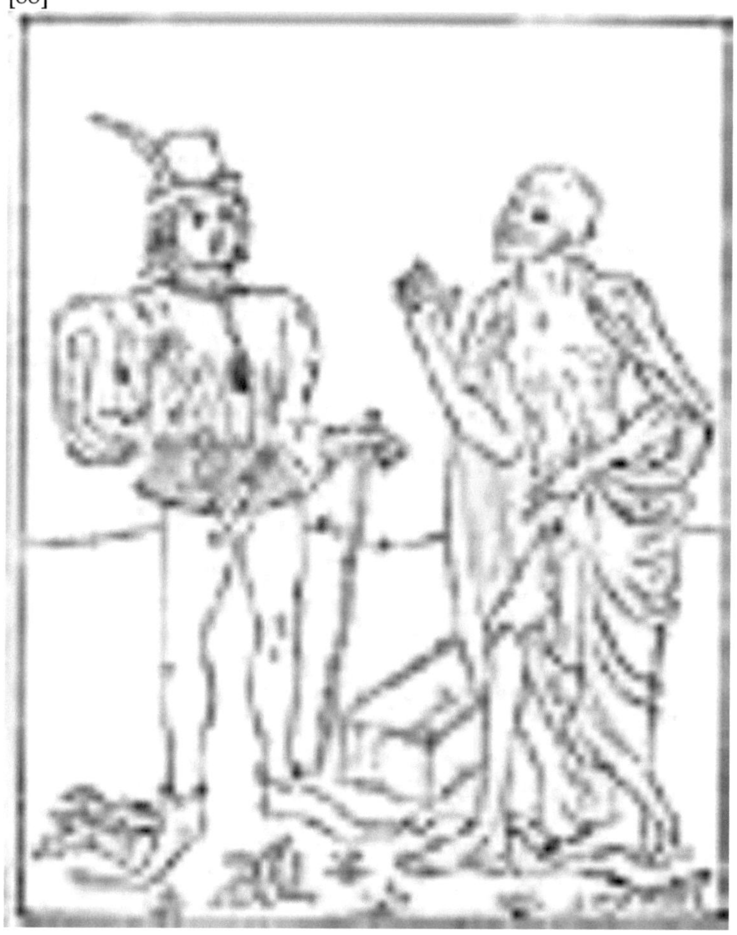

DEATH AND THE GALLANT. ToList

Several of Wyatt's iconoclastic blunders have been already mentioned; we now come to his chief iniquity. The **Hungerford Chapel**, demolished by Wyatt, stood at the east end of the building on the north side of the Lady Chapel, with which it was connected by openings cut in the main wall. This chapel was one of those of which Fuller so quaintly wrote, "A chantry was what we call in grammar an adjective, unable to stand of itself, and was therefore united for better support to some ... church." An addition to the building in a much later style, it was founded by Margaret (daughter and sole heir of William, Lord Botreaux,) in 1464; she was interred within its walls in 1477. Her history, too full to note here, is a sad one, the loss of her movable goods by "fyre" in Amesbury Abbey being but a small incident among her many troubles. A peculiarly interesting inventory of the ornaments and furniture that she gave to this chantry has been preserved; it is printed in Dugdale's "Baronage," vol. ii., p. 207, and also in "The Wiltshire Archæological Magazine," vol. xi. The chapel, in the somewhat florid late Perpendicular style, had a large east window of five lights, and three of triple lights in its north wall. The outside was adorned with shields and devices of the family, and crested with battlements. Within it had a richly-groined roof, and underneath a large arch cut in the north wall of the Lady Chapel, and therefore opening into the hall of the chantry, stood the monument of Lord Hungerford, surmounted by an ornamental four-arched canopy. This altar tomb, now devoid of the gold and colour that once enriched it, is in the nave. Its armour, "like a lobster," with its peculiar pattern, its large shoulders and elbow-pieces, and its jewelled girdle, is quoted by Meyrick as a very fine [89] example of its period. Above were eight niches of demi-quatrefoiled arches, with a fascia of quatrefoils surmounted by a cornice of oak leaves. Between the monument and the doorway was a series of wall-paintings of great interest. One, "Death and the Gallant," has been engraved, and the dialogue below it preserved. As the verses are archaic in spelling, it may be best to follow a more modern version ("Wilts Archæological Magazine," vol. ii., p. 95):

> "Alas, Death alas! a blissful thing thou were
> If thou wouldst spare us in our lustiness,
> And come to wretches that be of heavy cheer
> When they thee ask to lighten their distress.
> But out, alas, thine own self-willedness
> Harshly refuses them that weep and wail

To close their eyes that after thee do call.

Graceless Gallant in all thy lust and pride
Remember this, that thou shalt one day die,
Death shall from thy body thy soul divide —
Thou mayst him escape not certainly,
To the dead bodies (here) cast down thine eye;
Behold them well, consider too and see,
For such as they are, such shalt thou too be."

Of this Mr. Francis Douce, in his volume "The Dance of Death," says it was "undoubtedly a portion of the Macaber Dance, as there was close to it another compartment belonging to the same subject. This painting was made about the year 1460, and from the remaining specimen its destruction is greatly to be regretted, as judging from the dress of the young gallant the dresses of the time would be correctly exhibited."

There were other wall paintings, including a large St. Christopher with the Christ Child on his shoulder, and an Annunciation, said to have been a fine work. An interesting memorial of the chapel as it stood in the middle of the seventeenth century, is to be found in an MS. pocket-book, still preserved in the British Museum (Harl. MS. 939), which belonged to a Captain Symons, of the Royalist Army. When he visited Salisbury in 1644 he made many notes and sketches of the armorial bearings in this chantry.

The Beauchamp Chapel.—The interior view here reproduced from "Gough's Sepulchral Monuments of Great Britain" although not very clear is curiously interesting, conveying as it does trustworthy evidence of the building so wantonly swept away.

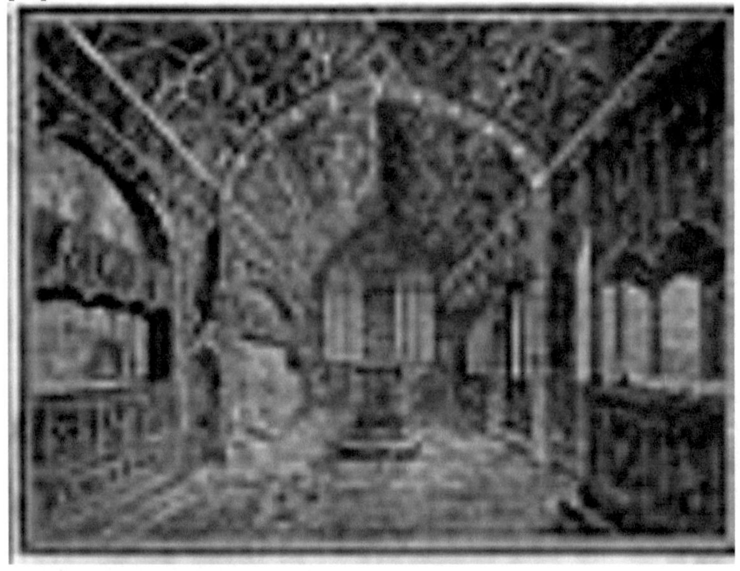

INTERIOR OF THE DEMOLISHED BEAUCHAMP CHAPEL.
ToList

Of the Beauchamp Chapel, on the south side of the Lady Chapel, there appears to be no exterior view extant, but from sketches of its interior, and descriptions, it must have been a fine specimen of its period, and worthy of its designer, the builder of St. George's Chapel, Windsor. It was larger and more elaborate in detail than the Hungerford chantry, but like it in plan, and similarly lighted by one large east window, and three in the side wall. The remains of its founder, Bishop Beauchamp, reposed in a plain tomb in the centre. In the wall on the north side were exquisite canopies above the tombs of the father and mother of the bishop. An altar tomb of Sir John Cheyne, now in the nave, stood formerly at the south-west corner (see page 48). There was a custom that on Christmas Day and all holy days the wives of the mayor and aldermen and gentry of the city, came to prayers in the Beauchamp chapel in the evening with flambeaux and torches, excepting on Innocents' Day, when they went to their own parish churches. In an interesting Guide to the Cathedral, now in the British Museum, annotated in the last century by some [91] visitor, we find an entry concerning this chapel, "The ceiling is of Irish oak, and never known to have spiders or cobwebs in it."

Much of the carved work in both these chantries was employed elsewhere in the buildings. The plea put forward for their removal was founded on a report by Francis Price thirty-six years before, wherein he considered them unsafe. When the Hungerford Chantry was added one of the outside buttresses of the Lady Chapel aisle was removed to make room for it; the opening pierced through the main walls of the cathedral into both the chapels were also sources of weakness. Wyatt seized upon these facts, and with the precedent of Price's report, declared the chapels unsafe, and also, which was no doubt his real motive for action, that "their lack of uniformity" injured the appearance of the buildings. Wyatt's ideal virtues were of the lowest order, to obtain neatness and tidiness he was prepared to sacrifice any and every thing, and the two chapels were obviously not in the style of the cathedral, nor, unluckily (for had they been they might yet be standing), precisely symmetrical in effect, so they were swept away. These actions at Salisbury, and similar destruction at Lincoln, Hereford, and elsewhere, have made Wyatt's name odious; but deserving though he be of all blame, it must not be forgotten that restorers of to-day, even at Salisbury, have effaced much interesting work of past time on the same pretext: that it failed to accord with the rest of the work to which it was obviously a late addition. This plea, specious and even excellent in theory, has probably done more irreparable injury to our ancient buildings than even the iconoclasts of the Reformation. A shattered ruin may convey a clear idea of its original state, while a smooth, pedantic restoration will obliterate it entirely.

The Stained Glass throughout the whole building survives but in a few instances, and these, with two exceptions, not in their original places. Of its wholesale destruction we have sad evidence extant in a letter, dated 1788, from John Berry, glazier, of Salisbury, to Mr. Lloyd, of Conduit Street, London. It may be transcribed in full, to show how reckless the custodians of the fabric were at that time:—
"Sir. This day I have sent you a Box full of old Stained & Painted glass, as you desired me to due, which I hope will sute your Purpos,

it his the best that I can get at Present. But I expect to Beate to Peceais a [92] a great deal very sune, as it his of now use to me, and we do it for the lead. If you want more of the same sorts you may have what thear is, if it will pay for taking out, as it is a Deal of Truble to what Beating it to Peceais his; you will send me a line as soon as Possoble, for we are goain to move our glasing shop to a Nother plase, and thin we hope to save a great deal more of the like sort, which I ham your most Omble servant—John Berry."

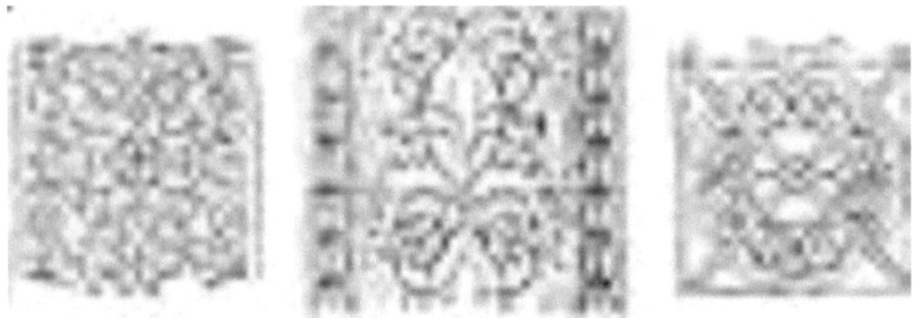

PORTIONS OF THE OLD STAINED GLASS. ToList

The fragments that survived were collected some fifty years since, and placed in the nave windows, and in parts of some of the others. The most important are in the great west triple lancet, wherein the glass ranges in date from the twelfth to the fifteenth century. Mr. Winston, in his Paper read in 1849 before the Archæological Institute and printed in the Salisbury volume for that year, considered that the earliest fragments are from a Stem of Jesse about 1240, and some medallions about 1270. He describes two of the ovals that are on each side of the throned bishop, a prominent figure in the lower half of the central light, one of the Christ enthroned, the other of the Virgin. The two medallions below them he believes represent "Zacharias in the Temple," and "The Adoration of the Magi." The later glass now in the same window may be either Flemish work brought hither from Dijon, or possibly partly from Rouen, and partly from a church near Exeter. It has been conjectured that in the south lancet the figures represent SS. Peter and Francis, in the central one the Crucifixion, the Coronation of the Virgin, and the Invention of the Cross, and in the north light the Betrayal of Christ and St. Catherine. In two of the [93] side windows of the nave are the arms of John Aprice (1555-1558) and Bishop Jewell (1562).

The stained glass in the north choir aisle includes a window executed by Messrs. Clayton and Bell, in memory of Archdeacon Huxtable, with figures of archangels and angels in the upper lights, and the Angel appearing to Gideon, and the Vision of Isaiah, in the lower panels. Also a window by Clayton and Bell to the memory of the wife of the Rev. Chancellor Swayne, having for its subject the reply of our Lord to his disciples. In the east side of the Morning Chapel is a window by Messrs. Burleson and Gryles to the memory of Mrs. W.R. Hamilton, with the Nativity, Crucifixion, Resurrection, and the three archangels, Gabriel, Michael, and Raphael.

In the south choir aisle are two Clayton and Bell windows, to the memory of George Morrison, and two others excellently treated, both designed by Holiday, and executed by Powell. In the one eight panels represent four holy women of the Old Testament, and the four Maries. This is to the memory of the late Countess of Radnor. In the other, to the memory of Jacob, the 4th Earl of Radnor, a similar screen of decoration embodies figures of eight prophets.

In the south-east transept is a window erected to the officers of the Wiltshire Regiment who fell in the Sutlej Campaign in 1845-6, and in the Crimean War of 1854-5; also one of "The Raising of Lazarus." In the upper windows of this transept is a quantity of old glass of different dates, which had been stored away for over a century in the roof of the Lady Chapel, until lately collected and placed where it now is.

The south choir aisle has a window in memory of the late Duke of Albany, "Jacob's Dream," and two of the intended six windows of a hierarchy of angels—the Angeli Ministrantes and the Angeli Laudantes—designed by Sir E. Burne-Jones, and executed by William Morris, which are notably among the most superb examples of the art of glass painting since mediæval times. Next in order towards the east is a window of fine design to the memory of the late Duke of Albany.

In the south-west transept there are three Clayton and Bell windows: in memory of Archdeacon Macdonald, with three subjects from the Life of Christ; in memory of Bishop Douglas, and in memory of C.G. Verrinder; also one to the [94] memory of Sir G.A. Arney, with Moses and the Tables of the Law, and the Sermon on the Mount; and the large south window, by Bell, to the memory of Dean Hamilton.

Above the altar is a fine light window of last century work, singularly good of its kind — bad though the kind may be.

In the south aisle of the nave is a window to the memory of Mr. W.M. Coates, with subjects, the miracles of healing, executed by Messrs. Clayton and Bell.

In 1890 a fine modern window, from a design by Henry Holiday, was inserted in the south aisle of the nave. This has for its subject, "Suffer little children to come unto me." It is to the memory of John Henry Jacob and his wife.

In 1620 Dr. Simpson mentions "three great windows newly glazed in rich colours to make the story of St. Paul."

Throughout the cathedral, and in the Chapter House, were many specimens of geometrical painted glass, some of which are figured in Mr. Winston's Paper, before referred to. These have served as motives for much modern design, which, faithfully as it may have copied the forms, has generally missed the softened colour that distinguishes the original work.

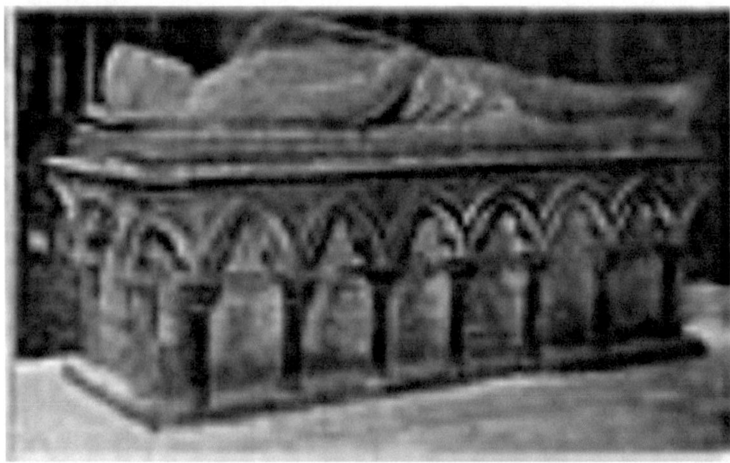

TOMB OF WILLIAM LONGESPÉE, 1ST EARL OF SALISBURY (P. 47).
From a Photograph by Catherine Weed Ward. ToList

[95]

HISTORY OF THE SEE. ToC

The site of old Sarum—Searobyrig, the dry city, as the Saxons called it—is about a mile to the north of the present New Sarum, or Salisbury, to use the more familiar name. It was probably a fortified place from very early times, long before it became the Roman station of Sorbiodunum. William of Malmesbury says that "the town was more like a castle than a city, being environed with a high wall, and notwithstanding that it was very well accommodated with other conveniences, yet such was the want of water that it sold at a great rate." This latter statement, although repeated by every chronicler, is not supported by investigations of recent explorers, who found an ample supply in divers wells. Francis Price concludes that "it was frequented by Roman Emperors from the coins of Constantine, Constans Magnentius, Crispus, and Claudius, being found frequently among its ruins." This statement also lacks probability. A legend of the visit of a single emperor might have been barely credible; but the lavish variety the otherwise trustworthy historian offers is fatal to one's belief. Its early history, more or less legendary, need not be chronicled here. Probably Kenric the Saxon, who captured it in 553, lived there, and it seems to have been kept in his line until Egbert united the whole Heptarchy. King Alfred ordered Leofric, Earl of Wiltunscire, to add to its fortifications, which appear to have fallen into decay after the Romans held it. In 1003 Svein, King of Denmark, pillaged and burnt it, but the religious establishments if not spared were soon re-established, for we find that Editha, Queen of Ædward [96] the Confessor, conveyed the lands of Shorstan to the nuns of St. Mary, Sarum. At this time it appears to have possessed a mint, as a coin of Ædward the Confessor bears an inscription showing that it was struck by Godred at Sarum.

From the time of St. Aldhelm, in 705, to that of Herman, in 1058, there are no other facts of its secular history sufficiently pertinent to our purpose to warrant their quotation here, as the record of the place is so woven into the lives of its bishops, that the brief summary of the ecclesiastics who held the see includes all we need of the history of the city. In this kingdom within a kingdom, a cathedral surrounded by a fortress, its inhabitants were naturally split into factions; the soldiers and the clergy failed to agree, and in spite of the document quoted below, there is little doubt that political rather than climatic reasons led to the removal of the cathedral. Whether, as some writers think, it was but an insignificant structure, it is certainly recorded that the church erected by Osmund took fifteen years to build. Five days after its consecration, on April 5th, 1092, it was partially destroyed by a thunderstorm. We find in Robert of Gloucester's "Chronicle" (Hearnes ed., p. 416) this allusion to the disaster:

> "So gret lytnynge was the vyfte yer, so that it al to nogte,
> The rof the Church of Salesbury it broute
> Rygt evene the vyfte day that he yhalwed was."

Whether the sentence in an old chronicler that Roger "made anew the church of Sarum" means it was so seriously damaged by the lightning that he actually rebuilt it, or merely that he restored it, is not clear. Roger was the great architectural genius of his time, and from the evidence of its ground plan, traced in the foundations revealed in the singularly dry summer of 1834, it may be that the stately edifice, 270 feet long by 75 feet wide, on the plan of a Latin cross, was in its last state not the work of Osmund. During the excavations at this time, various fragments of stained glass and several keys were discovered, also what was apparently the original grave of St. Osmund before his body was moved to Sarum. An extract from Harrison's "Description of Britain," prefixed to Hollinshed's "Chronicle" shows clearly enough the principal events that produced the crisis which doomed Old Sarum to desolation. "In the time of ciuile warres the souldirs of the castell [97] and chanons of Old Sarum fell at ods, inasmuch that often after brawles they fell at last to sadde blowes. It happened therefore in a rogation weeke that the cleargie going in solemn procession a controversie fell between them about certaine walkes and limits which the one side claimed and the other denied. Such also was the hot entertainment on eche part, that at last the Castellans espieing their time gate betweene the cleargie and the towne and so coiled them as they returned homewards that they feared anie more to gang their boundes for that year. Hereupon the peope missing their belly-chere, for they were wont to haue banketing at every station, a thing practised by the religious in old tyme, they conveyed forthwith a deadly hatred against the Castellans, but not being able to cope with them by force of arms, they consulted with their bishop ... that it was not ere the chanons began a church upon a piece of their own ground.... And thus became Old Sarum in a few years utterly desolate."

By other accounts we find there was insufficient room for all the canons to live within the walls, and the right of free egress being disputed the position became so intolerable, that Bishop Richard Poore, a man of great force of character, who succeeded his brother, took up the design Herbert had set aside, and commenced negotiations in earnest, the result of which is best explained by the following document:

"Honorius, bishop, Servant of the servants of God to our rev. brother Richard, bishop, and to our beloved sons the Dean and Chapter of Sarum, health and apostolical benediction. My sons the dean and chapter, it having been heretofore alleged before us on your behalf, that forasmuch as your church is built within the compass of the fortifications of Sarum, it is subject to so many inconveniences and oppressions, that you cannot reside in the same without corporal perils: for being situated on a lofty place, it is, as it were, continually shaken by the collision of the winds; so that while you are celebrating the divine offices, you cannot hear one another the place itself is so noisy: and besides the persons resident there suffer such perpetual oppressions, that they are hardly able to keep in repair the roof of the church, which is constantly torn by tempestuous winds. They are also forced to buy water at as great a price as would be sufficient to purchase the common drink of the country: nor is there any [98] access to the same without the licence of the Castellan. So that it happens on Ash Wednesday when the Lord's Supper is administered at the time of the Synods, and celebrations of orders, and on other solemn days, the faithful being willing to visit the said church, entrance is denied them by the keepers of the castle, alleging that the fortress is in danger, besides you have not there houses sufficient for you, wherefore you are forced to rent several houses of the laity; and that on account of these and other inconveniences many absent themselves from the service of the said church."

This mandate, dated at "the Lateran, 4th of the calend of April, in the second year of our Pontificat," concludes by giving formal power for the translation of the church to another convenient place.

After the cathedral was removed the prosperity of the place quickly waned. The new roads and bridges made access to the new city more convenient. Wilton suffered from the growth of its new rival, but Sarum ceased to be even a ruin, as the very stones of its cathedral were ultimately taken to build a wall around the precincts of the new church, and oblivion soon overtook the ancient city, which to-day is not even a hamlet, but at most a geographical expression. As a specimen of an early "burgh," or hill fortress, its form well deserves study. Its circular walls, and various ditches and ramparts, are shown in plans in the County History, in Francis Price's book, and elsewhere.

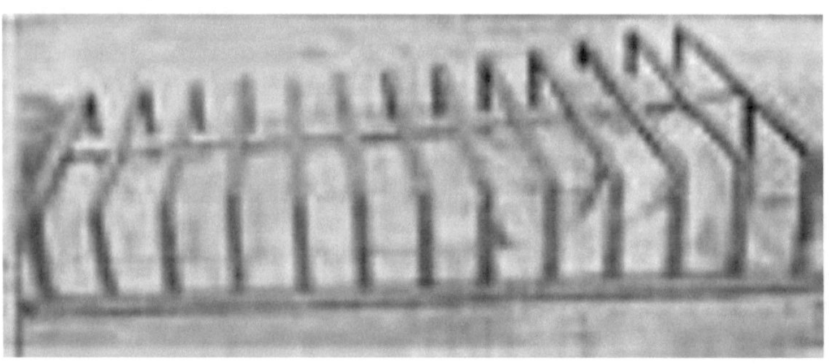

TOMB OF "THE BOY BISHOP" (P. 49).
From a Photograph by Catherine Weed Ward. ToList

[99]

THE DIOCESE OF SARUM.

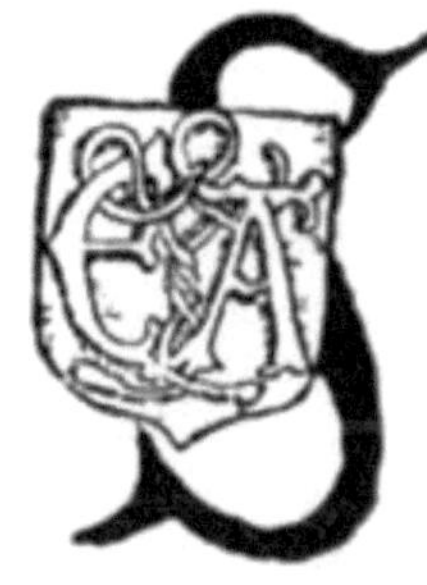

So far as its history concerns us here, it suffices to note that the greater part of Wiltshire, and those portions of Dorset and Somerset which had been comprised in the see of Winchester, were, about the year 705, during the reign of Ina, King of the West Saxons, included in the new diocese of Sherbourne, which in its turn, about two hundred years after, *circa* 905-9, was sub-divided into those of Wells, for Somerset, and Crediton, for Devon. About 920, a new see was allotted to Wiltshire, whose bishop took his title from Ramsbury, near Marlborough, on the borders of the county; and with this was soon after re-united the smaller diocese of Sherbourne, and in 1075, the episcopal seat was removed to the fortress of Old Sarum, whence in 1218 it was again removed to the present city. In 1542, part of the see was devoted to the new diocese of Bristol. The see of Sherbourne, ruled over by St. Aldhelm from 705 to 709, was a much larger one than the second diocese of the same name which in 1058 was united to Ramsbury, under Herman, who held it from 1058 to 1078. The eight previous bishops are more or less well known, and in the admirable "Diocesan History" and in the "Fasti Ecclesiæ Sarisburiensis," both by the late Rev. W.H. Jones, there is much interesting detail of the earlier rulers of the diocese now called Salisbury.

Herman, by birth a Fleming, was one of the ecclesiastics brought over by Edward the Confessor. His record is unmarked by events that left lasting results. He made a bold but fruitless attempt to annex the Abbey of Malmesbury. During his time, as an old writer quaintly phrases it, "it is agreed by all authors, both printed and in manuscript, that there was not yet [100] any cathedral, church, or chapter, either within or without the King's Castle [of Old Sarum], but only a chapel and a dean." Later authorities, however, assign to him the commencement, at least, of a cathedral. In Benson and Hatcher's "Wiltshire," we find it has been conjectured that Herman, on removing his see to Sarum, found there a chapel and a dean, and that in exchange for this building he transferred the two cathedrals of Sherborne and Sunning to the Dean to whose peculiar jurisdiction they have since belonged; other evidence, however, points to the church having been begun and finished by Osmund, his successor, whose own words in the charter of foundation run: "I have built the church at Sarum and constituted canons therein." An epistle of Gregory IX. to the bishops of Bath and Wells states that, "Osmund of pious memory had employed great care as well in temporals as in spirituals, so that he had magnificently builded the said church from its foundations and enriched it with books, treasures, ... and lands from his own property." Herman, like other English bishops who were his fellow-natives Leofric at Exeter, and Giso at Wells, was not deprived of his see after the Conquest; but in 1075, in obedience to the decree of the Council of London that bishops' sees should be removed from obscure to more important places, he chose the hill of Sarum. His remains are said to have been transferred to a tomb in the present cathedral, but later antiquarians decline to endorse the tradition.

Osmund, who is believed to have been the nephew of William the Conqueror, was son of Henry, Count of Seez, in Normandy; he was created Earl of Wiltshire soon after the Conquest, before he became an ecclesiastic; Camden speaks of him as the "Earl of Dorset." As the author of the "Consuetudinariam," the ordinal of offices for the use of Sarum, wherein he collated the various forms of ritual in use at many churches, both in England and on the Continent, he won a fame far more than the building of Old Sarum, were it never so stately a cathedral, could have secured him. His famous "Sarum Use" was adopted by almost the whole of England, and reflected glory upon the church that instituted it, so that in the words of an old historian, "like the sun in his heavens, the church of Salisbury is conspicuous above all other churches in the world, diffusing the light everywhere and [101] supplying their defects." The original manuscript of this great work is one of the choicest treasures of the cathedral library exhibited to those who have access to that collection; it is also available to the ordinary student in a volume entitled, "The Church of our Fathers," published by Dr. Rock in 1849. "As a man," says William of Malmesbury, "Osmund was rigid in the detection of his own faults, and unsparing to those of others." Although his body and his tomb were moved to the Lady Chapel of the new cathedral in 1226, and his name adored popularly, he was not canonized until over two hundred years later. Pope Callistus, the first of the Borgias, issued the bull on January 1st, 1456, but not, according to rumour, until ample funds had been supplied to facilitate his action. Some interesting correspondence relating to it has been lately printed in the "Sarum Charters and Documents," issued under the direction of the Master of the Rolls. The bull itself, in the keeping of the chapter, has been printed in Volume iii. of the great collection of Papal bulls edited by Cocqueline, and published in Rome, 1743. On July 15th, 1457, according to the authority of a writer in "Archæologia," Vol. xiv., the translation of his body was completed, principally at the expense of the bishop, a huge concourse of people being present at the festival. From the plentiful accounts of miracles worked at his shrine long before he was officially canonized, there is but little doubt but that it had become a favourite place of pilgrimage. He died in 1099, and in spite of his tomb being removed to the cathedral in 1226 and a stately shrine erected later, a stone with no inscription but a date of doubtful authenticity — MXCIX — is all that commemorates him there to-day.

The next bishop was **Roger**, who was elected in 1102, consecrated in 1107, and died in 1139. If his fame as an ecclesiastic is not so assured as that of his illustrious predecessor, in architecture and in secular history he has left a decided mark. He was a poor Norman priest, who won his mitre by singing a hunting mass quickly before Henry I. Made chaplain by the king on his accession, he afterwards became first chancellor, and then justiciary. He organized the Court of Exchequer, which has preserved the earliest official records known to us. His castles at Devizes, Sherborne, and Malmesbury excited the jealousy of the nobles; his son was [102] chancellor, one nephew Bishop of Ely, and another nephew Bishop of Lincoln. Besides much work, now destroyed, at Old Sarum (so that whether he merely restored the damage caused by lightning, or rebuilt it from the foundations, according to the Norman custom, we cannot tell), his additions to Sherborne Minster are still memorable as a new departure in Norman architecture; in fact, he has been called the great architectural genius of the thirteenth century. "Unscrupulous, fierce, and avaricious," he is a type of the great feudal churchmen when they were veritable rulers. According to William of Malmesbury, "was there anything contiguous to his property which might be advantageous to him, he would directly extort it either by entreaty or purchase, or if that failed, by force." Although after King Henry's death Henry, Bishop of Winchester, persuaded him to open the vast treasure of the late king to Stephen, yet in the fourth year of his reign Stephen imprisoned him, and the Bishop of Lincoln, his nephew, and seized their castles of Devizes and Sherborne, Newark, and Sleaford. Bishop Roger the same year, according to one chronicler, "by the kindness of death, escaped the quartan ague which had long afflicted him, and died broken-hearted." But another version says that "he starved to death through a promise to King Stephen that his castle of Devizes should be surrendered to him before he eat or drank; but his nephew, the Bishop of Ely, who then had possession of it, kept it three days before he made the surrender to the king."

Jocelin de Bohun, or, as he is sometimes called, de Bailleul (1142 to 1184), is best known from his quarrel with Thomas à Becket, of Canterbury. For his share in framing the "Constitutions of Clarendon," he was excommunicated by the archbishop. On the death of Roger, in 1139, King Stephen nominated Philip de Harcourt, but the canons preferred Jocelin, who was not, however, consecrated until 1142. After the murder of A'Becket he "purged himself by oath of his offences" towards his late foe. In 1184 he retired to a Cistercian monastery, and died shortly afterwards. A monument on the south side of the cathedral nave is attributed to him.

The see was now left vacant for five years, when Hubert Walter, was consecrated, in 1189; he shortly after went to the Holy Land to join Richard I. in his crusade. While at Acre he was nominated to the vacant archbishopric of Canterbury, to [103] which he returned in 1193. He exercised a powerful influence on both king and people; the latter, with whom he had never been popular, found at his death that "they had lost the only bulwark strong enough to resist or break the attack of royal despotism."

Herbert de la Poer, or Poore (1194-1217), who succeeded him, ruled in a troubled period, when the realm was under the interdict of Pope Innocent III. Compelled to quit Old Sarum, he died at Wilton in 1217.

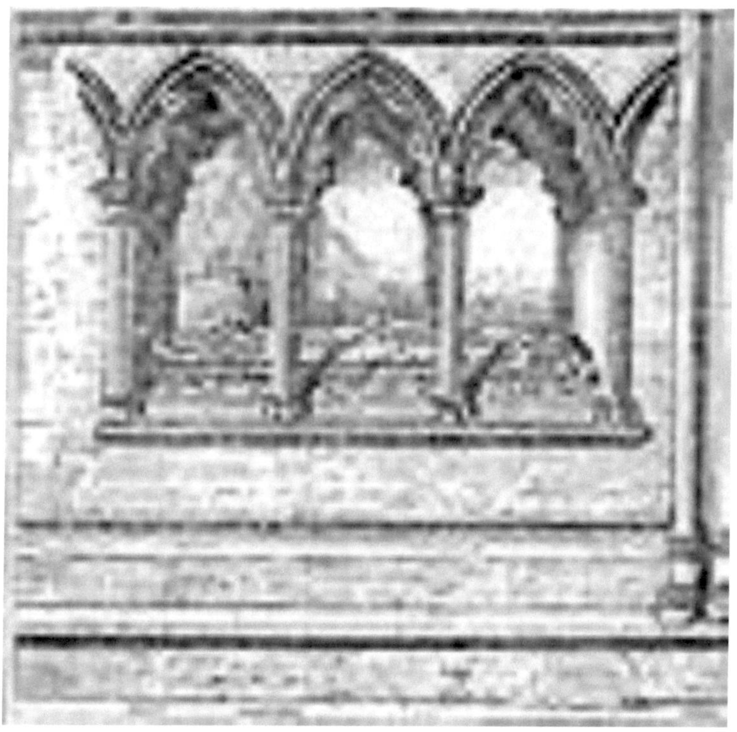

MONUMENT LOCALLY ACCREDITED TO BISHOP POORE.
ToList

With **Richard Poore**, who was consecrated Bishop of Chichester in 1215, and in 1217 Bishop of Old Sarum, where he had been dean, begins the record of the bishops immediately connected with the building. His history is so intimately bound up with that of the cathedral, that here it is sufficient to note that he ruled at Old Sarum and Salisbury until 1229, when he was translated to Durham. [10] His distinct influence upon the architecture of that cathedral, in connection with Elias de Derham, is noticed elsewhere. He died at his [104] birthplace, Tarrant (Tarent Crawford [11]), in Dorsetshire, where he had founded a Cistercian nunnery, in which his heart is said to have been interred; his body was taken to Durham, and a monument with his effigy erected in the new cathedral at Salisbury. The names of St. Osmund and Richard Poore stand out beyond all others in connection with this see. The one for the indirect glory he conferred upon it by his memorable ordinal; the other by his removal of the cathedral and the superb fabric he left to commemorate his fame. With them, excepting possibly Bishop Hallam, the record of men of mark ceases; of their successors hardly one has had a reputation beyond his diocese, and certainly there is not one whose fame has spread beyond his native land.

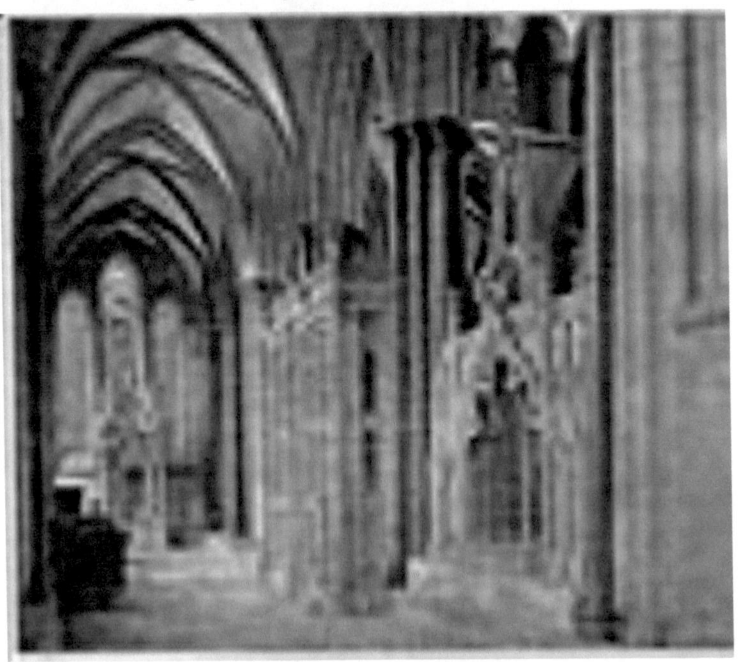

NORTH CHOIR AISLE, WITH BISHOP BINGHAM'S MONU-MENT. ToList

Robert Bingham (1229-1246) finished the work of the [105] cathedral during his eighteen years' rule; but when he died he left it in debt 1,700 marks. His monument, with effigy, is now in the north choir aisle.

144

William of York (1247-1256) was one of the chaplains to Henry II.; by his renewal of the vexatious custom of attending the lord's courts, he became very unpopular. Matthew Paris mentions him as one of the favourites of the king, and Bishop Godwin says that he was better versed in the laws of the realm than in those of God.

Giles of Bridport, or de Bridlesford (1257-1262), who held also the Deanery of Wells by a faculty "in Commendam," for Pope Honorius, continued the works of the cathedral until it was consecrated, in 1258, by Boniface, Archbishop of Savoy, the brother of the queen of Edward I. He also founded the college of Vaux. In 1260, during his bishopric, there is a curious entry in a document, lately printed, which refers to Nicholas of York, Canon of Salisbury, *Le engineur.*

In the same volume (Rolls Chronicles, 1891), there is a note of this bishop granting 200 lbs. of wax annually from his wardrobe for increasing the lights in the church, as he had been told that amount would be sufficient to double the number of the candles at each ministration.

Walter de la Wyle (1263-1271), the founder of the church of St. Edmund of Abingdon, has a mutilated effigy assigned to him in the cathedral.

Robert de Wykehampton (1274-1284), although elected by the canons, the monks of Canterbury, and the king, was opposed by the archbishop, who, after four years' interval and an appeal to Rome, was forced to consecrate him. He is said to have become blind in 1278.

Walter Scammel (1284-1286). Although on his election the monks of Canterbury appealed to the Pope against it, they subsequently withdrew their opposition. He was buried near the Audley Chapel.

Henry de Braundeston (1287), who died the same year, was buried, according to Leland, in the Lady Chapel.

Walter de la Corner (1289-1291) was one of the chaplains of the Pope. He was buried in the middle of the choir, "nearly under the eagle."

Nicholas Longespée (1292-1297) was fourth and youngest son of the first Earl of Salisbury, and Countess Ela.

[106] **Simon of Ghent**, or de Gand (1297-1315), first empowered the mayor and citizens to fortify the city. According to a document printed in the "Rolls Chronicles," 1891, the visitation of many of the churches, about 1300, compares badly with a similar record for 1220; ignorance of the clergy, gross neglect of the fabric, insufficient and dilapidated books and vestments, with other evidences of lack of energy, are very frequent.

Roger Mortival (1315-1330) founded a collegiate establishment at Knowsley, his birthplace. The Library of Merton College, Oxford, contains many manuscripts, his gift while he was Archdeacon of Leicester. He is said also to have drawn up the statutes by which the cathedral is still partly governed.

Robert Wyville, or Wivil (1330-1375), was, by Walsingham's account, not merely destitute of learning, but so deformed and ugly, "it is hard to say whether he was more dunce or dwarf, more unlearned or unhandsome," that had the Pope seen him he would never have endorsed his appointment. He was a militant bishop, and in 1355 instituted a suit against William de Montacute, and sent his champion clothed in white to try wager of battle with him. He recovered for his see 2,500 marks and the ancient castle of Old Sarum, also that of Sherborne. He obtained permission to fortify his manors of Sarum, Sherborne, Woodford, Chardstock, Potterne, Canning, Sunning, and his mansion in Fleet Street (now Salisbury Court), "in the suburbs of London." His brass is in the Morning Chapel.

Ralph Erghum (1375-1388) was probably of Flemish birth. He was translated to Bath and Wells in 1388, where he died in 1400. He is said to have erected the City Cross as a penance, but the Sarum register seems rather to indicate that he compelled the Earl of Salisbury to do so.

John Waltham (1388-1395) was Master of the Rolls in 1382, and Keeper of the Privy Seal in 1391. For a time he resisted the metropolitan visitation of Archbishop Courtney, notwithstanding that the Bishop of Exeter had been forced to yield in a similar contest, but when the archbishop excommunicated him he was compelled to submit. He was specially in the favour of his king, Richard II., and died Lord High Treasurer in 1305. He was buried ("not without much general dissatisfaction," according to Walsingham,) in Westminster Abbey, where his brass can be seen in the floor of the chapel of the Confessor, to the right of King Edward's tomb.

[107] **Richard Mitford** (1395-1407) was the favourite, and confessor of Richard II., but during the so-called "wonderful" parliament he was imprisoned in Bristol Castle, until released by the King on his re-assumption of power. In 1389 he was nominated to the see of Chichester, and translated therefrom to Salisbury in 1395. His tomb stands in an angle of the south transept.

Nicholas Bubwith (1407), at one time Treasurer of England, held Salisbury for three months only, between the bishoprics of London and Bath and Wells. He died at Wells, 1424.

Robert Hallam (1407-1417). Notwithstanding his brilliant career, both the origin and birthplace of this prelate are unknown. "Born in England of royal blood," says one chronicler, but there is no corroborative evidence. Prebendary of York, Archdeacon of Canterbury in 1401, Chancellor of Oxford 1403, he left England in 1406 for Rome, and was nominated by Pope Gregory XII. to be Archbishop of York; this latter preferment was withdrawn, but in its stead he became Bishop of Salisbury in 1407. He was at the Council of Pisa in 1409, and, in 1411, was created a cardinal by Pope John XXIII. At the famous Council of Constance, 1415-1417, he was one of the foremost champions of religious liberty, and almost alone in condemning the punishment of death for heresy. Indeed, the whole future of the Roman church is said to have been changed by his death at the Castle of Gotlieb in 1417, and the supremacy of the Italian party assured by the decease of its most formidable opponent. The brass that marks his burial place in Constance cathedral is supposed to have been executed in England, and sent thence some time after his death. It is engraved in Kites' "Monumental Brasses of Wiltshire."

John Chandler (1417-1426) is remembered chiefly for his brief life of William of Wykeham.

Robert Neville (1427-1438) was the nephew of Henry IV.; after holding the see of Salisbury for ten years he was translated to Durham. He founded the monastery at Sunning.

William Ayscough (1438-1450), who has left little record of his life, met his death during a local rising in 1450, the year of the Jack Cade rebellion. On the feast of SS. Peter and Paul his church at Edingdon, near Westbury, one of his palaces, was attacked by a mob, who seized the bishop in the vestments wherein he had just said mass, and, dragging him to [108] a hill-top near, there they stoned and beheaded him, stripping off his garments and dividing them among themselves for memorials. His body was afterwards interred at Edingdon. Possibly his scholarship, which separated him from his people, was the real cause of his unpopularity, which is, however, generally attributed to his frequent absence with King Henry VI., to whom he was Confessor.

Richard Beauchamp (1450-1481) was translated from the bishopric of Hereford. Son of Sir Walter, and grandson of Lord Beauchamp of Powick, he was sent on diplomatic missions to various courts, including Burgundy. In 1471 he was one of the signatories of the truce with the Duke of Brittany. In 1477 he became Dean of Windsor, and was appointed by Edward IV. master of the works then in progress, which included the rebuilding of St. George's Chapel. At Salisbury he left the great hall of the bishop's palace and his own superb chantry as memorials of his architectural skill. Elsewhere in this book is a fuller description of this beautiful tomb demolished by Wyatt. He himself was buried at Windsor; in an arch opposite his tomb was a missal carved in stone with a quaint inscription, beginning, "Who leyde this boke here." He is said to have been the first chancellor of the Order of the Garter, although Dr. Milner assigns that honour to William de Edingdon. Whether the first or not, he and his successors in the see held it by charter of Edward, until they were deprived in the reign of Henry VIII. In 1671 it was again awarded to the see of Salisbury, but passed, in 1836, with Berkshire to that of Oxford.

Lionel Woodville, or Wydville (1482-1484), nephew of Elizabeth, queen of Edward IV., was appointed to the see in 1482. His brother-in-law, the Duke of Buckingham, was beheaded in Salisbury market place just before the battle of Bosworth. Woodville is said to have died of grief occasioned by the downfall of the fortunes of his house on the accession of Richard III.

Thomas Langton (1485-1493) is best remembered as a patron of literature, for which he has been called a second Mæcenas, yet, despite the "fostering hand he always afforded to learned men," he was an opponent of Wicklif's heresies, and did his best to stamp them out in his see when they had gained a number of adherents.

[109] **John Blyth** (1494-1499) was Chancellor of Ireland in 1499. An effigy, assumed to be his, is in the north transept.

Henry Dean, or Denny, or Syer (1500-1501), was translated to Canterbury shortly after his appointment to Salisbury. He is believed to have been one of the victims of the Great Plague, and to have died at Lambeth in 1503.

Edmund Audley (1502-1524) was Bishop of Rochester in 1480, translated to Hereford in 1492, and to Salisbury in 1502. His beautiful chantry still remains in its original position. St. Mary's, Oxford, contains a pulpit said to be his gift.

Lorenzo Campegio, Cardinal of St. Anastatius, was nominated by Pope Clement in 1524. He was sent to England to join Cardinal Wolsey in adjudicating upon the royal divorce. In 1535, when Henry VIII. disgraced Wolsey, Campegio was also deprived of his see by Act of Parliament. At Rome, however, he was regarded as Bishop of Salisbury until his death; and "for some time after" an independent succession was maintained by the Pope in two English bishoprics, namely, Salisbury and Worcester.

Nicholas Shaxton (1535-1539) was President of Gonville Hall, Cambridge, and for a while a sturdy supporter of the king. At the time of Latimer's resignation he also resigned in common with many other bishops. He was imprisoned, and in 1546 condemned to be burnt, for denying the real presence; but recanting became prominent as opponent of the reformers, preaching fiery sermons at the martyrdom of Anne Askew and others. After he resigned his see he became suffragan to the Bishop of Ely. He died at Cambridge in 1556.

John Capon, or **Salcote** (1539-1557), had been Bishop of Bangor. His record is notorious for its greed and time-serving. First orthodox, then Protestant, and one of the revisers of the Liturgy under Edward VI., again changing under Mary, and one of the judges at the trial of Bishop Hooper of Gloucester. Fuller impeaches him with Veysey, or Harman, of Exeter, saying, "it seems as if it were given to binominous bishops to be impairers of their churches."

Peter Peto (1557), a cardinal nominated by the Pope, was refused possession by Queen Mary, who appointed Francis Malet, Dean of Lincoln, in his stead, but he in turn, before his consecration, was ejected by Elizabeth, who had succeeded to the throne meanwhile.

[110] **John Jewel** (1560-1571) is one of the few Protestant bishops connected with this see who can claim more than diocesan fame. He was born at Berry Narbor, Devonshire, in 1522, and appears to have belonged to a good old family. When a Fellow of Corpus, at Oxford, his adherence to the doctrines of the Reformation caused him to be expelled; but so greatly was he beloved for his pure life and his profound scholarship there, that in spite of his expulsion he was chosen to be Public Orator at his University. His life is too widely known to need an epitome here. Among his writings, the most famous, the "Apology for the Church of England," published in 1562, was quickly translated into every language in Europe. In episcopal matters he took great interest, and built the library over the cloisters, [12] besides devoting great care to the education of students, having always a number of poor lads in his house, and maintaining others at Oxford, one of whom was the famous "Judicious Hooker." Fuller praises him in terms that seem, however extravagant, to be generally admitted by his contemporaries to be fully deserved, and the famous sentence, "It is hard to say whether his soul or his ejaculations arrived first in heaven, seeing he prayed dying, and died praying," shows that he was reverenced by the Reformed Church as a veritable saint. He died at Monkton Fairleigh in 1571, his tombstone, despoiled of its brass, is now near that of Bishop Wyvil, whence it was removed from its former place in the choir.

Edmund Gheast, or **Gest** (1571-1577), the first Protestant Bishop of Rochester, was translated to Salisbury, where he gave a fine collection of books to the new library of the cathedral. His tombstone is in the north choir aisle.

John Piers (1577-1589) preached before Queen Elizabeth at the solemn thanksgiving for the defeat of the Spanish Armada. He was translated to York in 1589.

John Coldwell (1591-1596), a physician before he became a cleric, is also noticeable as the first married bishop who held the see. He was accused of wasting its revenues, and is responsible for the loss of Sherborne Castle, which he alienated, says Fuller, "owing to the wily intrigues of Sir Walter Raleigh."

Henry Cotton (1598-1615) was one of the chaplains of Elizabeth, and a godson of the Queen, of whom she is reported to have remarked that "she had blessed many of her godsons, now one should bless her." Sir John Harrington says, "he [111] had nineteen children by one wife, which is no ordinary blessing, and most of them sonnes. His wife's name was Patience; the name of which I have heard in few wives, the quality in none." As the second married bishop he certainly appears to have supported fully the Protestant opposition to the celibacy of the clergy.

Robert Abbott (1615-1618) was the elder brother of George, Archbishop of Canterbury. Fuller says, "George was the more plausible preacher, Robert the greater scholar; George the abler statesman, Robert the deeper divine. Gravity did frown in George, and smile in Robert." As one might infer from so strong an opponent of Laud, amid the large number of his published works most are polemical and Anti-Romish.

Martin Fotherby (1618-1620) held the see but a year, and hence left no lasting impression upon it.

Robert Townson (1620-1621), who attended the execution of Sir Walter Raleigh, and has left a graphic and touching account of his last hours, was but ten months bishop when he died, says Fuller, who was his nephew, of a fever contracted by "unseasonable sitting up to study," when preparing a sermon to preach before Parliament.

John Davenant (1621-1641) attended the Synod of Dort at the bidding of James I., and was the author of many theological works.

Brian Duppa, or **de Uphaugh** (1641-1660) was tutor to the sons of Charles I., and appointed to Salisbury just before the Commonwealth; he was deprived almost immediately, and lived in seclusion at Richmond until, at the Restoration, he was translated to Winchester. His memorial tablet is in Westminster. Of him Izaak Walton said, "he was one of those men in whom there was such a commixture of general learning, of natural eloquence, and Christian humility, that they deserve a commemoration by a pen equal to their own, which none have exceeded."

Humphrey Henchman (1660-1663) was appointed at the Restoration, no doubt as a reward for his great services to King Charles after the battle of Worcester. After holding the see three years he was translated to London.

John Earles (1663-1665), appointed Bishop of Worcester at the Restoration, was translated to Salisbury in 1663. One [112] of his books, "The Microcosmographie, or a Piece of the World Discovered in Essays and Characters," first published anonymously in 1628, was extremely popular, and ran through many editions; it is still read as a faithful picture of its times. Hallam in his "Literary History" praises it highly, Clarendon in his "Memoirs" also eulogizes its author, and Izaak Walton in his "Life of Hooper" speaks of his innocent wisdom, sanctified learning, and pious, peaceable, and primitive temper. Earles was constantly with Prince Charles during his exile, and hence one of the first ecclesiastics to receive preferment.

Alexander Hyde (1665-1667) was first cousin to the famous Lord Chancellor Clarendon. A portrait, alleged to represent this prelate, was found by Bishop Fuller in an obscure cottage; it is now in the Bishop's palace.

Seth Ward (1667-1689), who was made Bishop of Exeter at the Restoration, and translated to Salisbury in 1667, took great interest in the fabric, and restored the bishops' palace. The survey of the cathedral by Sir Christopher Wren was undertaken by his request and at his own cost. He regained for his see the Chancellorship of the Order of the Garter, lost for a century and a half. He founded the College of Matrons, and at his death at Knightsbridge in 1688, was buried in the south choir aisle. Dr. Walter Pope's biography of this bishop is an interesting record of an eventful life.

Gilbert Burnet (1689-1715). Lord Macaulay has summed up the character of this bishop in terms, that if they convey an impression of a vain, indiscreet, and somewhat blundering partisan, yet do justice to the vigour and strength of his character, while of the "History of his Own Times," and many other volumes yet remembered, he says: "A writer whose voluminous works in several branches of literature find numerous readers one hundred and thirty years after his death, may have had great faults, but must also have had great merits."

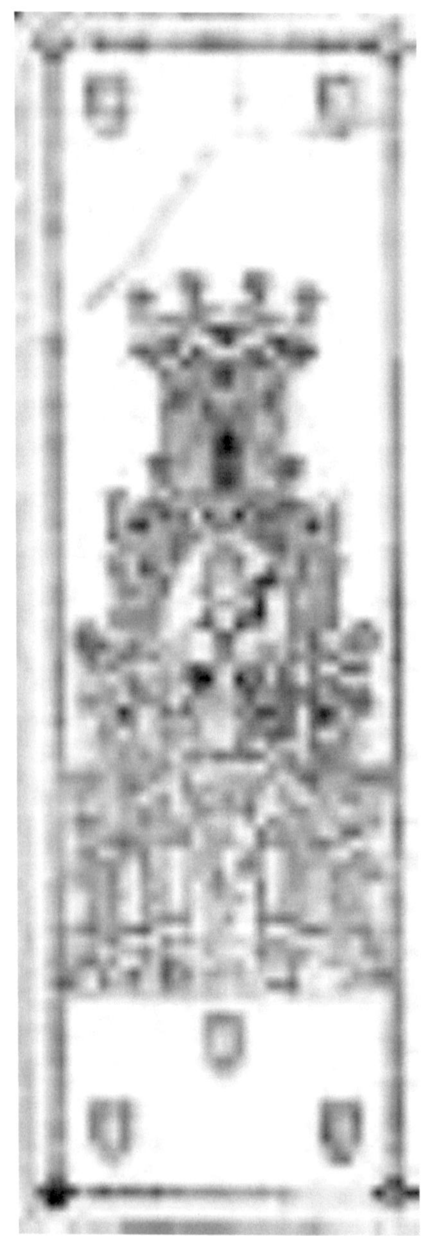

BRASS OF BISHOP WYVILLE
(*see* P. 66). ToList

William Talbot (1715-1721) was of the house of Shrewsbury, and father of Lord Chancellor Talbot. He was translated to Durham in 1721.

Richard Willis (1721-1723) held the see for two years, when he was translated to Winchester.

Benjamin Hoadly, Bishop of Bangor 1716, Hereford [113] 1721, Sarum 1723. Owing to the controversy raised by one of his sermons, Convocation was suspended for 150 years.

Thomas Sherlock (1734-1748) was appointed to Bangor in 1727, translated to Salisbury in 1734, declined the Archbishopric of Canterbury in 1747, and was translated to London in 1748. In the most apathetic time of the Anglican Church he is a striking example of activity and earnestness.

John Gilbert (1749-1757) was a turbulent bishop whose record is full of disputes with the civic authorities at Salisbury.

John Thomas (1757-1761), Bishop of Peterborough 1746, and afterwards Bishop of Winchester, was married four times, and is reported to have said that he had killed three wives by never contradicting them.

Robert Hay Drummond (1761) was translated to the Archbishopric of York four months after his appointment to Salisbury. He preached at the coronation of George III.

John Thomas (1761-1766), elected Bishop of St. Asaph in 1743, but consecrated to Lincoln, was eighty years old when translated to Salisbury.

John Hume (1766-1782), Bishop of Bristol 1756, Bishop of Oxford and Dean of St. Paul's 1758.

Shute Barrington (1782-1791), translated to Durham. Excepting Bishop Wilson, his fifty-six years' tenure of office is the longest in the Anglican Church. He died in 1826.

John Douglas (1791-1807) was present as an army chaplain at the battle of Fontenoy, in which he very nearly took an active part, but was so laden with valuables left in his care by officers, that he was compelled to refrain and be content to remain a non-combatant, and remove his treasures to a safe place. As author of "The Criterion, or Rules by which True may be distinguished from Spurious Miracles," 1754, and many other books, he established for himself a sound literary reputation. Made Bishop of Carlisle in 1787, and translated to Salisbury in 1791; he was also Dean of Windsor from 1780 to his death, when he was buried in St. George's Chapel.

John Fisher (1807-1825). Exeter, 1803, Preceptor to Princess Charlotte.

Thomas Burgess (1825-1837). St. David's, 1803.

Edward Denison (1837-1854). Brother of a late Speaker of the House of Commons, Viscount Ossington.

Walter Kerr Hamilton (1854-1869). Author of a [114] "Letter on Cathedral Reform," which followed his exhaustive contribution to the Cathedral Commission Reports, 1853.

George Moberley (1869-1885). Head Master of Winchester, 1835-1866.

John Wordsworth (1885).

FOOTNOTES:

[10] 14th May, 1228. *Vide* "Hist. Dunelm. Script.," App. lii.

[11] Others say Tarrant Monkton.

[12] This statement is open to doubt.

[115]

THE CLOSE AND CHURCHES.

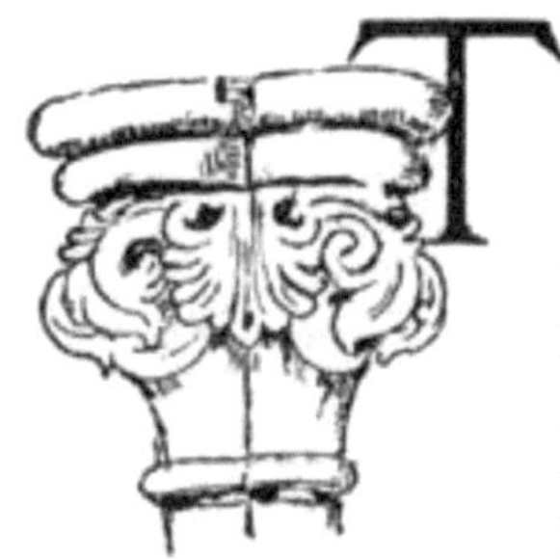

he **King's House**, which faces the west front, on the western side of the Close, is a stately building, wherein, tradition says, monarchs have dwelt. Richard III. is said to have been housed there when the Duke of Buckingham was brought prisoner to Salisbury; and in the reign of James I. its owner, Sir Thomas Sadler, was often honoured by visits from that monarch. Underneath the great gateway which pierces the building, in the north wall, is the shaft of a "sack lift," a curious relic of mediæval times. The fine proportions and sturdy treatment of the architecture of this house deserve study. It is now used as a training establishment for school mistresses. Close by is the Deanery, and to the south a building known as the **Wardrobe House**; which name is supposed to indicate its use in connection with the King's House; still farther south is **Leden Hall** (or Leyden Hall), hidden behind trees, so that from the Close you can but catch a glimpse of the building by Elias de Derham, to which reference has been made earlier in this book. In the other direction are the **Theological College**, a very lovely and spacious building, the **Choristers' School**, and many private houses of great antiquity and considerable beauty. Indeed, it is possible that at no other place could you find such a display of English domestic architecture, from mediæval to Georgian times. The beauty of the Close, well wooded as it still is, despite the havoc wrought by the terrible gale in March, 1897, is not to be put into words. No matter how praise were lavished in a description, it would yet be inadequate. But whether you see it for the first time, or after many visits, it still keeps its place as the most perfect thing of its sort in the world.

[116] The **High Street Gate**, which from its position may be regarded as the chief entrance to the Close, is an embattled structure of two stories, built, as the pieces of Norman stone work clearly

show, from material brought from Old Sarum. In the niche above the arch on the south side is a figure, popularly supposed to represent Charles I., although its proportions more nearly resemble those of James I. It is said that a statue of Henry III. originally occupied the niche. To the left, as you have passed the gateway, stands the picturesque **Matron's College** founded and endowed by Bishop Seth Ward in 1685. Also on the left is a house formerly occupied by Canon Bowles, and still earlier by Archdeacon Cole, both Salisbury worthies with more than local reputation.

St. Ann's Gate is in the east wall of the Close, in the southern angle. It is a long, low two-storied building, with two light perpendicular windows in the upper story, and from the street outside, where a projecting window is a noticeable feature, is very picturesque. In common with the other gates and with the walls of the Close, Norman stones moulded and carved are visible in many places. A house near the south side was occupied by Fielding, who moved afterwards next door to the Friary in St. Ann's Street, and finally to another at Milford Hill, where he wrote "Tom Jones."

Harnham Gate near the south boundary is but a fragment, an embattled archway devoid of an upper story. Near this gateway, just outside the precincts, stood the ancient college of De Vaux, founded in 1260 by Bishop Bridport.

The Bishop's Palace is not visible from the Close, but can be seen through a doorway in the cloisters. It is set in the midst of delightful gardens, a rambling picturesque building dating from many periods. Bishop Poore began it—Bishop Beauchamp built its great hall; within its walls are portraits of all the bishops of Salisbury since the Restoration.

The Hospital of St. Nicholas is situated between Harnham Gate and Harnham Bridge. The charter of its endowment dates from the castle of Old Sarum in September, 1227. It still shelters a dozen inmates in a most picturesque house, part of the original structure. On an islet is a more modern building, which is on the foundation of the chapel of St. John, suppressed at the Reformation.

The Church House, as it is now called, was formerly [117] known as Audley House, and belonged to the Earl of Castlehaven who was beheaded in 1631, and his property divided between the bishop and others. It is most picturesquely placed by Crane Bridge.

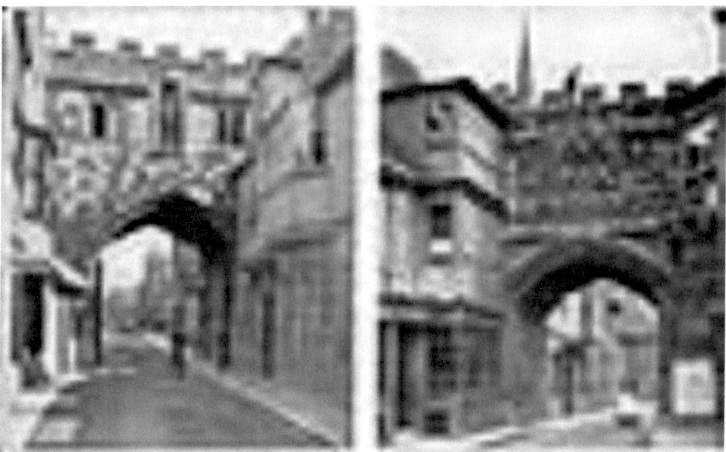

SOUTH FRONT.   HIGH STREET GATE.   NORTH FRONT.
From Photographs by Carl Norman and Co. ToList

The Poultry Cross is still standing near the Market Place. At one time a sundial and ball crowned the structure, but these have been replaced by a cross. Close by it and scattered frequently throughout the streets of the city are overhanging houses that betray their antiquity at a glance.

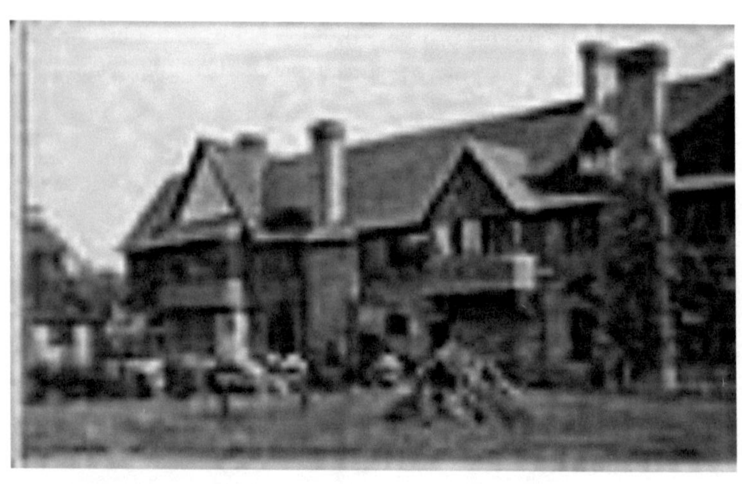

THE CHURCH HOUSE.

The Guildhall, a very interesting building as engravings show, was demolished at the end of the eighteenth century. The Joiners Hall, the Tailors Hall, the Hall of John Halle, the Old George, are still standing, with some of their features modified but not sufficiently altered to deprive them of interest.

The Church of St. Thomas à Becket is a most picturesque structure, and, placed as it is in a square of old tiled houses, makes a delightful picture. It consists of a nave with two aisles, a chancel with aisles, and a vestry room. It was built in 1240 by Bishop Bingham. The embattlemented tower has in its south front two niches containing much mutilated [118] figures of the Virgin and Child and St. Thomas à Becket. In the porch is a very curious panel with a biblical subject rudely carved by Humphrey Beckham, who died, aged eighty-eight, in 1671, and left this as his memorial. The most striking feature of the interior is the large painting above the chancel arch, representing the Day of Judgment, in the naïve manner of its [119] time. A reproduction will be found in Hoare's "Modern Wiltshire" (vol. 6), and most works on ecclesiastical mural decoration mention it as one of the most important examples that have come down to us. Other paintings in the south aisle were brought to light by Mr. G.E. Street during the restoration in 1867. Without and within it is a building hardly less worth study than the cathedral itself.

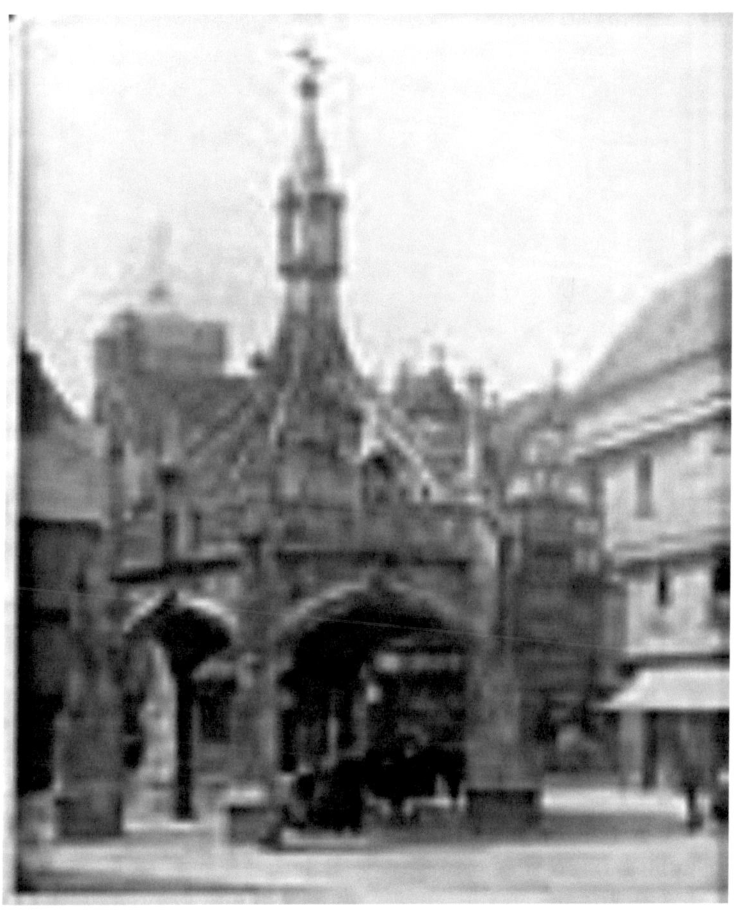

THE POULTRY CROSS.
From a Photograph by Carl Norman and Co. ToList

St. Edmund, founded by Bishop de la Wyle in 1268 for a Provost and twelve secular canons, is at the north-east of the city. To the east of its churchyard is the college of St. Edmunds, on the site of the convent founded in 1268 by the same bishop. In the grounds of the college stands the old north transept porch of the cathedral, a picturesque ruin whose architecture at once disposes of the theory that it came from Old Sarum.

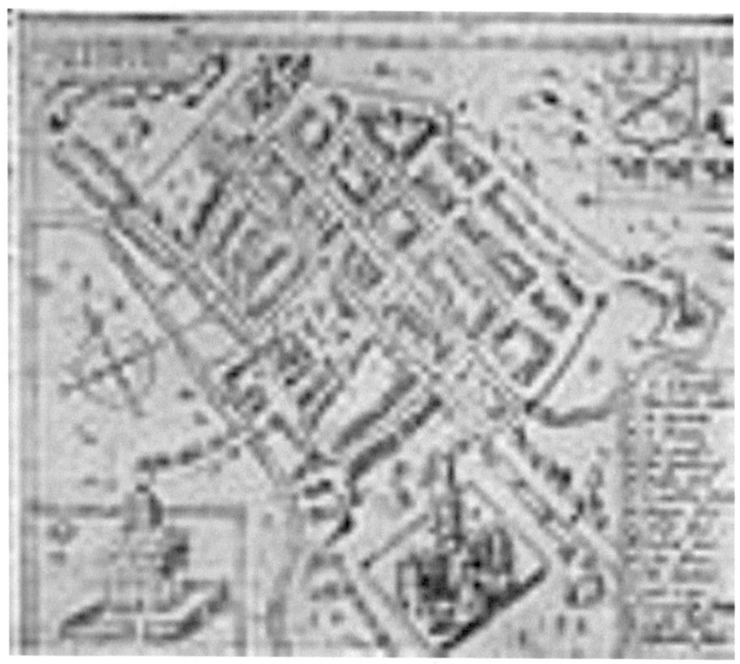

OLD PLAN OF SALISBURY. ToList

St. Martin is another church of very ancient foundation, containing an interesting Norman font.

[120] It is impossible to close even the most brief note of objects of interest at, or near, Salisbury, without naming George Herbert's church, Bemerton, and Stonehenge; two places which attract pilgrims from all parts of the world. Yet no space is left to describe them, or to refer to Henry Lawes, musician, and Philip Massinger, dramatist, two of the many famous men who had the city for their birthplace. The cathedral has been the main object of this volume, and other matters, interesting though they may be, must needs be left untouched here.

164

THE END.

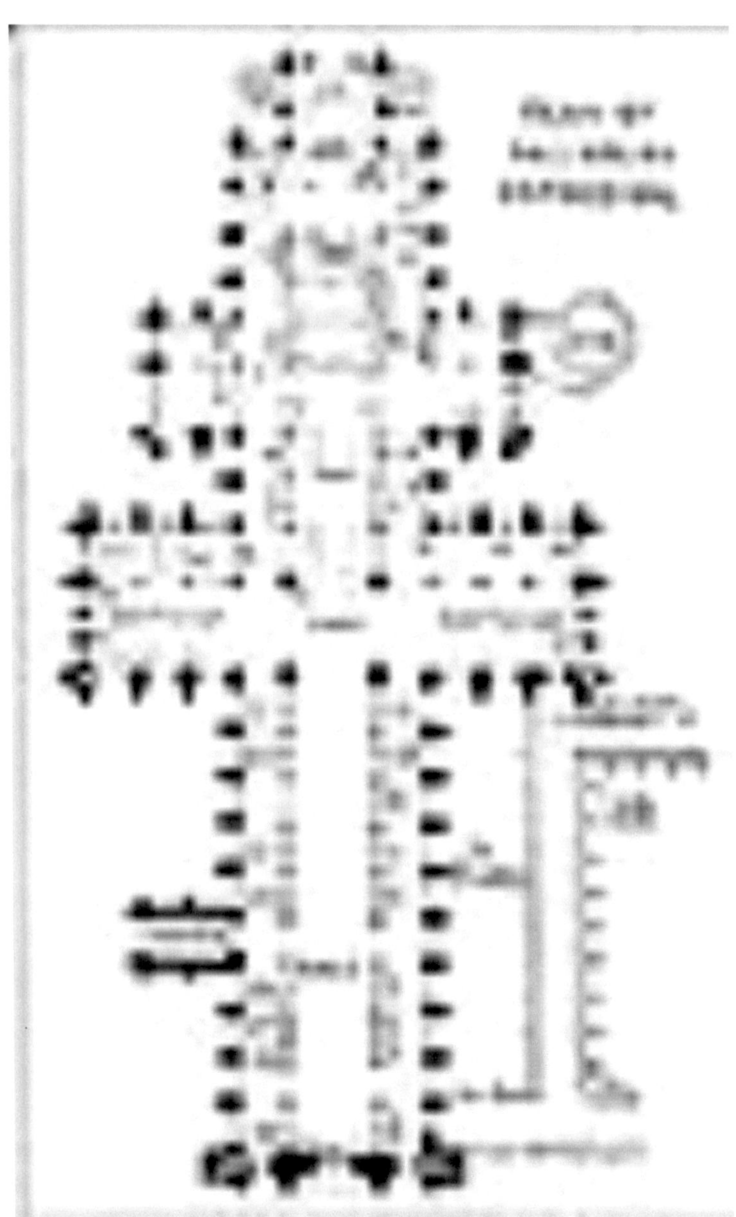

PLAN OF SALISBURY CATHEDRAL.